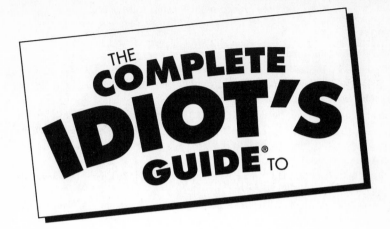

Fun FAQs

by Sandy Wood and Kara Kovalchik

ALPHA

A member of Penguin Group (USA) Inc.

Dedicated to our three favorite physicians: Marcia Anne Johnson, Vinod Kumar Kohli, and the late Everett Newton Rottenberg.

ALPHA BOOKS

Published by the Penguin Group

Penguin Group (USA) Inc., 375 Hudson Street, New York, New York 10014, USA

Penguin Group (Canada), 90 Eglinton Avenue East, Suite 700, Toronto, Ontario M4P 2Y3, Canada (a division of Pearson Penguin Canada Inc.)

Penguin Books Ltd., 80 Strand, London WC2R 0RL, England

Penguin Ireland, 25 St. Stephen's Green, Dublin 2, Ireland (a division of Penguin Books Ltd.)

Penguin Group (Australia), 250 Camberwell Road, Camberwell, Victoria 3124, Australia (a division of Pearson Australia Group Pty. Ltd.)

Penguin Books India Pvt. Ltd., 11 Community Centre, Panchsheel Park, New Delhi—110 017, India

Penguin Group (NZ), 67 Apollo Drive, Rosedale, North Shore, Auckland 1311, New Zealand (a division of Pearson New Zealand Ltd.)

Penguin Books (South Africa) (Pty.) Ltd., 24 Sturdee Avenue, Rosebank, Johannesburg 2196, South Africa

Penguin Books Ltd., Registered Offices: 80 Strand, London WC2R 0RL, England

International Standard Book Number: 978-1-59257-754-5
Library of Congress Catalog Card Number: 2007941480

10 09 08   8 7 6 5 4 3 2

Interpretation of the printing code: The rightmost number of the first series of numbers is the year of the book's printing; the rightmost number of the second series of numbers is the number of the book's printing. For example, a printing code of 08-1 shows that the first printing occurred in 2008.

Printed in the United States of America

Note: This publication contains the opinions and ideas of its authors. It is intended to provide helpful and informative material on the subject matter covered. It is sold with the understanding that the authors and publisher are not engaged in rendering professional services in the book. If the reader requires personal assistance or advice, a competent professional should be consulted.

The authors and publisher specifically disclaim any responsibility for any liability, loss, or risk, personal or otherwise, which is incurred as a consequence, directly or indirectly, of the use and application of any of the contents of this book.

Most Alpha books are available at special quantity discounts for bulk purchases for sales promotions, premiums, fund-raising, or educational use. Special books, or book excerpts, can also be created to fit specific needs.

For details, write: Special Markets, Alpha Books, 375 Hudson Street, New York, NY 10014.

Publisher: *Marie Butler-Knight*
Editorial Director: *Mike Sanders*
Senior Managing Editor: *Billy Fields*
Senior Acquisitions Editor: *Paul Dinas*
Development Editor: *Julie Bess*

Production Editor: *Kayla Dugger*
Copy Editor: *Jan Zoya*
Cover and Book Designer: *Kurt Owens*
Layout: *Brian Massey*
Proofreader: *Aaron Black*

Contents at a Glance

Contents

Introduction

When we signed on to write *The Complete Idiot's Guide to Fun FAQs*, we didn't realize how difficult it would be. Because questions and answers are our specialty, we were psyched about the project. But the title left us flummoxed, because the very nature of trivia is at odds with the concept of Frequently Asked Questions.

We decided to incorporate standard questions with several tangential ones that straddled the line of trivia. Of course, the notion that some of these questions are "trivial" precludes them from falling into the realm of being "frequently asked." As a result, these may not be FAQs in the truest sense. The entries here neither have the typical numeric layout nor the all-encompassing nature of other FAQ lists you've seen. We hope you'll still respect us in the morning.

And although this is our third book for Alpha Books' *Complete Idiot's Guide* series, we still like to believe that our readers are far from idiots. So, when you whittle things down, the title of this book should be *Fun Questions.* But would you buy a book called *Fun Questions?* (If so, let us know, and we'll write one.)

In the meantime, we hope that you enjoy this book. Better yet, use the material herein to show off in the office break room or to one-up that know-it-all uncle who drives you nuts at every family gathering. Won't that feel good?

Best regards,

Kara and Sandy

pigpencil.com

Acknowledgments

Thanks to Frances Fahey Kovalchik and Karl Kovalchik for their research assistance.

Thanks to Alison, Ellen, and Paul at Stonesong Press.

Thanks to the staff of Borders Bookstore and Seattle's Best Coffee in Birmingham, Michigan.

Thanks to Bill, Jerry, and Susan.

Trademarks

All terms mentioned in this book that are known to be or are suspected of being trademarks or service marks have been appropriately capitalized. Alpha Books and Penguin Group (USA) Inc. cannot attest to the accuracy of this information. Use of a term in this book should not be regarded as affecting the validity of any trademark or service mark.

ENTERTAINMENT

Academy Awards

Has the design/composition of the Oscar statuette changed over the years?

The only change of note was a temporary one from 1942–1944, when plaster statues were handed out to conserve metal for use during World War II.

What's the award's full name?

The Academy Award of Merit.

What is the Oscar statuette made of?

An alloy known as britannium, which is more than 90 percent tin. It's then plated with 24-karat gold.

Is an Oscar like a regular trophy?

Yes, but a bit heavier—an Oscar weighs about 8.5 lbs.

How much is an Oscar statuette worth?

In metal, maybe $150. But the Academy owns the rights to the statuettes and has the right to buy them back for $1 each if they're ever offered for sale.

Who walked away with the most Oscars at a single ceremony?

Technically, Walt Disney. To celebrate the success of his first full-length animated feature, *Snow White and the Seven Dwarfs*, Walt received one full-sized Oscar statuette and seven smaller ones.

Has any winner lost his or her Oscar statuette?

Yes. In fact, Meryl Streep lost hers before even leaving the 1980 ceremony. While in the restroom of the Dorothy Chandler Pavilion, she set it down and then forgot to retrieve it.

Who was the first animated character to co-host the Oscars ceremony?

Donald Duck, in 1958.

Has an actor ever mistakenly been given an Oscar?

No. Rumors began circulating that Jack Palance read the wrong name when Marisa Tomei was the surprise winner of the 1993 Best Supporting Actress Oscar for *My Cousin Vinny*. (Price Waterhouse Coopers reps are always in the wings to prevent such errors.)

When did a naked man disrupt the Academy Awards ceremony?

April 2, 1974. The fad known as "streaking" was in full swing (no pun intended). Somehow a man named Robert Opal made it past security and dashed across the stage in his birthday suit, flashing a peace sign just as host David Niven announced presenter Elizabeth Taylor.

Who was the first female Oscar winner to wear trousers (instead of an evening gown) to the ceremony?

Best Supporting Actress winner Julie Christie showed up at the 1966 Academy Awards in a gold lamé pantsuit, the first high-profile female to be so daring.

Elvis or The Beatles?

Who was once managed by Andreas Cornelis van Kuijk?

Elvis. Cornelis van Kuijk was born in the Netherlands, but immigrated to America as a teenager and changed his name to Tom Parker. While he was an Army veteran, he wasn't a real colonel; he was given that honorary title in 1948 for helping Jimmie Davis in his effort to be reelected governor of Louisiana.

Who had the most number-one pop **Billboard** *hits?*

The Beatles, who scored 20 chart-toppers in their career while Elvis managed only 17. The Beatles also scored six consecutive number-one hits in the mid-1960s, while Elvis managed only five in a row a few years prior.

Who met the president of the United States?

Elvis, who arranged a session at the White House with Richard Nixon in 1970. In fact, Presley spoke disparagingly of The Beatles during the meeting. He accused them of promoting "an anti-American theme."

Did Elvis and The Beatles ever meet in person?

Yes, once, on August 27, 1965, at Presley's home in Bel Air, California. Ringo Starr later summed up the four-hour session with his usual candor: "I felt I was more thrilled to meet him than he was to meet me."

Who hit the **Billboard** *Hot 100 and Top 40 the most times?*

Elvis, by a long shot. An amazing 154 of the King's songs appeared on the Hot 100, more than double that of The Beatles with 73. Likewise, Presley scored 104 Top 40 hits, compared to 52 for The Beatles.

Who embarked on a concert tour of the Far East in the mid-1960s?

The Beatles. Notwithstanding a three-city stint in Canada in 1957, Elvis Presley never toured outside the United States. Colonel Parker didn't hold a U.S. passport, so he couldn't travel overseas.

Who recorded more songs made popular by the other?

That's tough to say. Elvis's official live albums include renditions of "Hey Jude," "Something," and "Yesterday." While The Beatles played a few Elvis songs live or "just for fun" in the studio, none were officially released while the band was still together.

Who organized and operated an official fan club?

The Beatles. Brian Epstein helped form the organization in 1962 as a way to control (and profit from) the popularity of the band. While Elvis Presley Enterprises does bestow the "official" moniker on fan clubs, the King's management didn't operate its own.

Who had their own number-one Billboard *single replaced at the top spot by one of their new singles?*

Both. Elvis did it in 1956, when "Love Me Tender" replaced "Hound Dog" at the top of the chart. The Beatles repeated the feat eight years later in 1964, when "She Loves You" knocked "I Want to Hold Your Hand" off the peak.

Popular Movies

How many characters did Frank Morgan play in The Wizard of Oz?

Five: Professor Marvel, the Emerald City gatekeeper, the "horse of a different color" carriage driver, the Wizard's guard, and the Wizard himself.

What famous line was nearly censored out of Gone with the Wind?

Rhett Butler's "Frankly, my dear, I don't give a damn." Producers paid a $5,000 fine to ensure it would stay in the movie. Just to be safe, they filmed an alternate version, with Clark Gable uttering the milder "Frankly, my dear, I just don't care."

Were Sesame Street *pals Bert and Ernie named after characters in* It's a Wonderful Life?

No. While this rumor has persisted for years, Muppeteer Jerry Juhl states that it was just a coincidence.

What notable word is surprisingly never mentioned in the 1972 film The Godfather?

Mafia. The Italian American Civil Rights League had insisted that the word be removed from the script.

Who portrayed Darth Vader in the Star Wars *films?*

Several people. David Prowse was the man inside the costume, but James Earl Jones provided the voice. Anakin Skywalker (who became Lord Vader) was portrayed by Sebastian Shaw, Jake Lloyd, and Hayden Christiansen.

What's unusual about the shapely, stocking-clad legs in the famous poster for The Graduate?

They don't belong to the film's star, Anne Bancroft. Those gorgeous gams are attached to then-model (and future *Dallas* star) Linda Gray.

What is the name of that catchy tune whistled in The Bridge on the River Kwai?

It's called "The Colonel Bogey March." During World War II, American soldiers often chanted made-up anti-Hitler lyrics to well-known tunes. Such a version of this song was popular with U.S. soldiers.

Has an "adult" film ever won a Best Picture Academy Award?

Yes. Best Picture winner *Midnight Cowboy* was given an X rating (for nudity and violence) back in 1969, before that designation became synonymous with the porn industry.

Was Gene Kelly really "singin' in the rain" during his famous dance routine in the film of the same name?

No, it wasn't rain. It was a mixture of water and milk spat out from sprinklers. The liquid needed a bit of cloudiness to show up better on film.

How many times was the "F-bomb" dropped in Goodfellas?

Two hundred forty-six.

Songwriters

Did Barry Manilow write his signature hit, "I Write the Songs"?

Ironically, no. That number-one pop tune was written by Bruce Johnston of the Beach Boys. Manilow also did not write his other two number-one singles, "Mandy" and "Looks Like We Made It."

What New York building is famous for giving many songwriters (including Neil Diamond, Carole King, Burt Bacharach, and Neil Sedaka) their start?

The Brill Building, at 1619 Broadway. That's where music impresario Don Kirschner set up shop in 1958 with the intent of employing a stable of songwriters to churn out large quantities of pop hits.

What songwriter nearly died when the Andrea Doria *sank in 1956?*

Mike Stoller was aboard the cruise ship when it collided with the *Stockholm* off the coast of New York. Stoller and his wife were rescued, and learned upon arriving in New York that their song "Hound Dog" had become a huge hit for someone named Elvis Presley.

Why are most Beatles songs credited to Lennon-McCartney?

When John and Paul first started cutting class as teenagers to hang out and play guitar together, the pair made a "gentleman's agreement" that any song either of them composed would be credited to both of them.

What was Tin Pan Alley?

Out-of-tune pianos were called "tin pans" in the late nineteenth century. Around 1900, the sound of multiple pianos being played by songwriters at several music-publishing companies in the same Manhattan neighborhood led the area to become known as Tin Pan Alley.

What hit song from 1962 was written by Gong Show host Chuck Barris?

"Palisades Park" by Freddie "Boom Boom" Cannon. Barris penned the tune while working behind the scenes at *American Bandstand* (and possibly serving as a government hit man), and it hit number three on the *Billboard* pop chart.

How did Elton John and Bernie Taupin establish their famous writing partnership?

Both men answered a "songwriters wanted" ad placed in Britain's *New Music Express*. They worked together for six months before they ever met face to face; Bernie wrote batches of lyrics and mailed them to Elton, who then set them to music.

What inspired The Rolling Stones' Mick Jagger and Keith Richards to begin writing their own songs?

The band had focused on cover versions until Mick and Keith watched John Lennon and Paul McCartney sit down in the studio in 1964 and compose "I Wanna Be Your Man" in only half an hour. Jagger told Richards, "If they can do that, we should be able to do it, too."

Country and Rap

Why do we call it country and western?

It's a combination of the music played by people living in the rural Appalachians in the East (country) and the cowboy songs of the American frontier (western). The two styles converged into a unique American sound.

And why do we call it rap?

Because the lyrics are typically spoken—like in a rap session, where feelings are expressed by someone and criticized or supported by listeners.

What is the distinguishing factor in bluegrass music?

Bluegrass is to country what folk is to rock—they're related but not the same. It's characterized by the use of only select instruments, usually banjo, fiddle, guitar, and mandolin.

And what's the distinguishing factor in hip-hop?

In a nutshell, hip-hop is about the music, whereas rap is about the words. If the focus is on the vocalist doing the rapping, it's a rap song. If the tune is more prominent, it's hip-hop.

Has any artist managed to make both the country and rap Top 40?

Yes. The Pointer Sisters, who hit number 37 on the country chart back in 1974 with "Fairytale," then went on to score several Top 40 hits on the R&B/rap charts in the 1980s.

Why is Hank Williams Jr. sometimes called Little Bocephus?

He earned the name as a youngster due to his resemblance to a ventriloquist dummy used by performer Rod Brasfield, who was once a regular at the Grand Ole Opry.

Which musical genre sells the most albums, rap or country?

The two were neck-and-neck in the early 2000s, but country music has held its ground while rap sales dipped nearly 20 percent in 2006 alone.

What was the first rap song to hit number one on the pop charts?

It all depends on your definition of "rap," but the most widely accepted answer is the 1981 single "Rapture" by Blondie.

Was Louis "Grandpa" Jones really a grandpa?

Eventually, yes. But he began playing the curmudgeonly character on the radio in the mid-1930s, when he was only in his 20s.

What's this whole "M.C." and "D.J." thing?

M.C. stands for Master of Ceremonies—the person on the mic. The D.J. is the disc jockey, the person performing the vinyl record scratching that's a common part of rap music.

Classical and Opera (for the Unfamiliar)

Music from what opera was used as the basis for the musical "Hamlet" episode of Gilligan's Island?

George Bizet's *Carmen.*

Wasn't one of those songs from Carmen *also the theme for the 1976 film* The Bad News Bears?

Yes, "The Toreador Song."

What's the proper name of the song often played at graduation ceremonies?

"Pomp and Circumstance," written by Edward Elgar.

What two children's songs use the tune from Mozart's "Ah! Vous Dirai-Je, Maman"?

"The Alphabet Song" and "Twinkle, Twinkle, Little Star."

Why did British citizens whistle the opening four notes to Beethoven's Fifth Symphony during WWII?

To let others know they were Allies. The sound was also used by the BBC to signify victory, because the Morse code for "V" was dot-dot-dot-dash.

What's the name of the fast-paced song that often accompanies jugglers or plate-spinners?

"The Sabre Dance," written by Aram Khachaturian.

Who recorded the Top 10 song "Hooked on Classics" in 1981?

That was the Royal Philharmonic Orchestra conducted by Louis Clark, who also enjoyed pop success working with the Electric Light Orchestra.

Speaking of ELO, did the band ever perform true classical pieces?

Live, yes. And tinges of popular classics appeared in the band's recordings, best exemplified by the album *Eldorado* (subtitled *A Symphony by the Electric Light Orchestra*).

What about the music used in the Warner Brothers cartoon, **What's Opera, Doc?**

Those tunes were opera compositions written by Richard Wagner, the guy who also wrote "The Bridal Chorus" ("Here Comes the Bride").

The music for what popular sing-along tune was lifted from Gilbert and Sullivan's **The Pirates of Penzance?**

"Hail, Hail, the Gang's All Here." The tune was borrowed from the song "With Cat-Like Tread."

Animation

Is it true that Mel Blanc, who voiced Bugs Bunny, was allergic to carrots in real life?

No, but he didn't care for the flavor. He chewed real carrots in order to achieve the "perfect" sound, but spit them out instead of swallowing them.

What word was censored from several episodes of Beavis and Butthead *after they originally aired?*

"Fire." Beavis's fascination with flame supposedly inspired at least one Ohio youngster to set fire to a mobile home.

What comic strip led to The Flintstones *being given a new name?*

Hi & Lois. The couple's name was Flagston, which producers felt was too similar to Fred and Wilma's original last name, Flagstone.

Why do many cartoon characters have only three fingers and a thumb on each hand?

It makes it easier for the artists and saves paint in the coloring process. It also looks more natural, because cartoon characters' features are outlined in black, and too many fingers makes the hand look cluttered.

Why did the name of Popeye's archenemy change from Bluto to Brutus?

Bluto was used in the original Fleischer Studios cartoons. Later, King Features Studio mistakenly thought that Bluto was a trademark of Fleischer, so in their *Popeye* cartoons, the name was changed to Brutus to avoid potential legal issues.

What was the first animated film also nominated for a Best Picture Oscar?

The 1991 Disney feature *Beauty and the Beast.*

How much were The Beatles paid for providing their voices to the animated feature film Yellow Submarine?

Nothing, because their voices were performed by actors. In fact, other than recording some new songs for the movie, they wanted nothing to do with it until they saw a nearly finished print. Pleased with the result, they decided to film a short live segment to end the movie.

What cartoon show was taken off the air due to consumer complaints that it was nothing more than a long commercial?

Linus the Lionhearted. Featuring Post cereal characters including Sugar Bear, the show was pulled by the FCC in 1969.

Who provided the voice of Woody Woodpecker?

For more than 30 years, Woody was performed by Gracie Lantz, the wife of the character's creator, Walter Lantz. She chose not to receive credit for the role, because she feared kids would be disappointed to know that a woman was behind the voice.

Did Wile E. Coyote ever catch the Road Runner?

In a 1980 made-for-TV short, the cunning coyote did manage to grab hold of the Road Runner's leg. He then held up a sign asking the audience, "Now what do I do?"

What product was heavily promoted in the original broadcast of A Charlie Brown Christmas?

Coca-Cola. The references were removed for future airings.

What cartoon sidekick wore nothing but a bowtie and a smile?

Yogi Bear's pal, Boo Boo.

"Radio" Songs

Only 10 songs with "radio" in their titles have hit the Top 40 in the rock era. Can you identify the artists for each?

1. *"Life is a Rock (but the Radio Rolled Me)"?*
   Reunion, #8 in 1974.

2. *"On the Radio"?*
   Donna Summer, #5 in 1980.

3. *"Radio Ga Ga"?*
   Queen, #16 in 1984.

4. *"Radioactive"?*
   The Firm, #28 in 1985.

5. *"Nothing on but the Radio"?*
   Gary Allan, #32 in 2004.

6. *"Radio Romance"?*
   Tiffany, #35 in 1989.

7. *"Song on the Radio"?*
   Al Stewart, #29 in 1979.

8. *"Turn Up the Radio"?*
   Autograph, #29 in 1985.

9. *"Video Killed the Radio Star"?**
   The Buggles, #40 in 1979.

10. *"You Turn Me On, I'm a Radio"?*
    Joni Mitchell, #25 in 1973.

* While this song wasn't a huge radio hit, it did notch a place in pop-culture history as the first video played on MTV when the network premiered on August 1, 1981.

What "radio" song got Elvis Costello banned from Saturday Night Live *for 12 years?*

"Radio Radio." Elvis and The Attractions were scheduled to play "Less Than Zero" on a 1977 broadcast, but Costello stopped after the first line of the song and continued with "Radio Radio" instead. Not amused, *SNL* producers had the band removed from the studio.

TV Theme Songs

"Final Frontier" was the title of the theme song for what TV show?

No, it wasn't *Star Trek*, but *Mad About You*.

What famous film composer's early credits include the quirky theme to the 1960s sci-fi TV series Lost in Space?

John Williams, who went on to score many of the most popular film series in history, including *Star Wars* and *Indiana Jones*. As a side note, young Billy Mumy (who portrayed the role of young Will Robinson on the show) went on to form the musical act Barnes and Barnes, best known for the novelty song "Fish Heads."

What was the title of the funky theme for Sanford & Son?

"The Streetbeater." The tune was composed by music legend Quincy Jones.

Who wrote the theme song for The Tonight Show?

Canadian singer/songwriter Paul Anka revamped an old song called "Toot Sweet." Johnny Carson added a drum riff so that he'd get a co-writing credit. The pair split $400 in royalties every time the show aired, for 32 years, 5 nights a week. You do the math.

On some TV shows, a cast member sang the show's theme song. Can you identify the singers and shows for these five themes?

1. *"Eyes of a Ranger"?*
   Chuck Norris, from *Walker, Texas Ranger.*

2. *"I'm a Survivor"?*
   Reba McEntire, from *Reba.*

3. *"New Girl in Town"?*
   Linda Lavin, from *Alice.*

4. *"There's No Place Like Home"?*
   Marla Gibbs, from *227.*

5. *"The Unknown Stuntman"?*
   Lee Majors, from *The Fall Guy.*

Who sang the theme song for Happy Days?

For the first two seasons of the series, Bill Haley's "Rock Around the Clock" was the opening theme, while "Happy Days" by Pratt and McClain played over the closing credits. By season three, the Pratt and McClain song was a hit single and took over as the show's main theme.

Why don't most current TV shows use a theme song?

Network executives fear that those 30 seconds of music might bore the audience and prompt them to change the channel. Starting the show immediately and running the credits over the action is an attempt to hold on to viewers. Theme-song licensing agreements have also become prohibitively expensive.

What is the title of the Jeopardy! *"think" music?*

It's called "Time, for Tony." Tony is the son of *Jeopardy!* creator
Merv Griffin, who wrote the ditty as a lullaby for the boy.

Who whistles the theme song on The Andy Griffith Show?

Earle Hagen, the man who wrote the tune, is also the one who
whistles it. The song is called "The Fishin' Hole."

Did Desi Arnaz write the I Love Lucy *theme song?*

Even though his character claimed to have written it as a gift for
his wife in the episode "Lucy's Last Birthday," the show's theme
was in fact composed by Eliot Daniel and Harold Adamson.

Classic Rock and Pop

Was the original Beatles White Album *really just plain white?*

Yes and no. While the earliest covers featured the album's real
title (*The Beatles*) embossed in white, they were also machine-
numbered in black ink. Later editions were unnumbered, but gray
lettering replaced the embossed text.

What was the first single to be certified platinum?

"Disco Lady" by Johnnie Taylor. This doesn't mean it was the first single to sell a million, however. It was just the first one to do so after the RIAA introduced the platinum award in 1976.

What album was the first rock LP to include the lyrics in its packaging?

Sgt. Pepper's Lonely Hearts Club Band by The Beatles.

What was the first album by Chicago not to be named with a number?

Technically speaking, it was the band's debut, titled *Chicago Transit Authority*. The next one to fit this description was *Hot Streets* (which would have been *Chicago XII*).

Are these five Australian musical acts really Australian?

AC/DC?

Yes and no. The band was formed in Australia, but its key original members—vocalist Bon Scott and brothers Angus and Malcolm Young—were all born in Scotland.

Olivia Newton-John?

No. She was born in England, but moved with her family to Australia when she was five years old.

Men at Work?

Most of the band members were Australian, but lead singer Colin Hay was born and raised in Scotland before moving to Australia as a teenager.

The Bee Gees?

No. Like Olivia, they moved to Australia as youngsters, but the three brothers (Barry and twins Robin and Maurice) were born on the Isle of Man off the British coast.

INXS?

Not as much as they once were. The band was formed in Sydney in 1977, but lost focus after the death of lead singer Michael Hutchence. His replacement, highlighted on the reality show *Rock Star: INXS*, was Canadian vocalist J. D. Fortune.

Is Michael Jackson's Thriller *still the biggest-selling album in American history?*

No, that honor currently belongs to *Eagles: Their Greatest Hits 1971–1975. Thriller* dropped to number two on the list in the year 2000.

What's the proper title of the fourth Led Zeppelin album?

It has no official title, but is commonly referred to as *Led Zeppelin IV*, the *Runes* album, and *Zoso* (four letters that resemble the symbols on the album's cover).

What about the best-selling album in UK history?

Across the pond, the 1981 *Greatest Hits* album by Queen is the biggest ever, with more than 5.5 million copies sold.

What date is considered the beginning of the rock era?

July 9, 1955. That's the day Bill Haley and the Comets hit number one on the *Billboard* chart with "Rock Around the Clock."

What is the shortest song to have hit number one on the U.S. pop chart?

"Stay" by Maurice Williams and The Zodiacs, which clocks in at a brief 1 minute and 37 seconds.

What is the most repetitive song title to have topped the **Billboard** *chart?*

"(Shake, Shake, Shake) Shake Your Booty," which hit number one in 1976 for KC and the Sunshine Band.

LIFE **2**

Babies

What is colic?

Doctors believe that it's not a gastric problem, but a symptom of a baby's underdeveloped nervous system. The only way for a baby to relieve the sensory overload from the highly stimulative environment surrounding him is to cry. And cry. And cry.

Why are babies so darned cute?

Anthropologists have identified certain characteristics that they call "cute cues": large, bright, forward-facing eyes; a large, round head; and a chubby body. It is believed that human infants evolved with these traits because they evoked a nurturing and protective instinct in mothers.

Is my baby really smiling at me, or is it just gas?

Until about two months of age, babies smile when they're feeling content, not as a reaction to external stimuli. So, yes, it's gas.

What is "tummy time"?

For infants, too much time spent lying in one position can cause plagiocephaly (a misshapen head). So while babies often lie on their backs, they should also spend some time on their stomachs (under parental supervision, of course).

What is the APGAR score?

It's the result of a five-part test given to newborns at one minute of age, and then again at five minutes. A perfect score is 10; anything below 7 calls for additional testing.

And where did the APGAR name come from?

It's both the name of the procedure's developer (Dr. Virginia Apgar) and an acronym for the steps taken in the test: Appearance (skin color), Pulse, Grimace (reflexes), Activity (muscle tone), and Respiration.

What causes pregnancy cravings?

Doctors believe they are the body's way of alerting mothers to nutritional deficiencies. The old "pickles-and-ice-cream" stereotype is rooted in fact—pregnant women require more sodium and calcium, which would make them crave both salty foods and dairy products.

Why do all babies have pug noses?

The bone that forms the nasal bridge doesn't develop until later. Baby has to squeeze through the birth canal, so a Jimmy Durante–style honker wouldn't make it any easier for Mom during labor.

At what age will my baby recognize my face?

About three months. Until then, any stranger with a face and hairstyle similar to Mom's will elicit a reaction.

Why are babies able to coo before they babble?

The "coo" sounds that come from the back of the throat are made with very little effort. Babbling ("dada," "baba") requires use of the tongue and the mouth, which need effort and control that takes time to develop.

Pets

Do pet food descriptions have any special meaning?

Any pet food that has some sort of qualifier in its name, such as "Liver Platter" or "Beef Nuggets," is required by U.S. law to contain 25 percent of the meat listed. Cans with more straightforward descriptions (like "Tuna for Cats") are required to contain 95 percent of the named ingredient.

Why does my dog tilt his head when I speak to him?

Canine eyes are set farther apart in their skulls than human eyes, so Fido sees what's around him more than what's right in front of his nose. He turns his head in order to see you better.

Why does cat urine smell so strong?

Cats were originally desert animals, so they require far less water than most other mammals. As a result, their urine is extremely concentrated, and rather pungent.

Where do hamsters come from?

No, not hamster trees. All golden hamsters in captivity today can trace their roots back to a litter (a mother and her 12 babies) found in Syria in 1930. Hamsters once ran wild there, but farmers hunted them to near-extinction.

What were the 10 most common cat names in the United States in 2006?

1. Tigger
2. Tiger
3. Max
4. Smokey
5. Sam

6. Kitty
7. Sassy
8. Shadow
9. Simba
10. Patch

Is it true that one dog year equals seven human years?

No. The average works out closer to four years. And while smaller breeds may not show signs of old age until 10 to 13 years old, larger breeds may begin to feel geriatric at age 8.

Why are poodles given those frou-frou haircuts?

They were originally bred as water retrievers, and most of their fur was shaved off to provide ease of movement when collecting prey. Strategic tufts were left in certain spots to keep the heart, lungs, hips, and leg joints warm.

Why isn't there a mouse-flavored cat food commercially available?

Because humans—not cats—buy pet food. That's why feline cuisine comes in such varieties as tuna, turkey, and beef; these are all foods that pet owners find palatable.

Which sex of parakeet is easier to train to talk?

Males. They mimic sounds in the wild as part of their mating ritual to attract females, so male parakeets are more amenable to repeating "pretty bird" than the ladies are.

Can I keep the goldfish I won at the fair in that cute little bowl?

No. A 10-gallon tank is needed to keep the fish healthy. Goldfish are actually better suited for ponds than for aquariums.

Elections and Voting

Is it true that German came within one vote of becoming the official language of the United States?

No. It came within one vote of being considered as an option in a congressional bill that would have chosen a national language. No such vote occurred, and even if it had, English would have been the preferred choice.

What organization has been promoted by MTV as a way for the "new generation" to get involved in politics?

Rock the Vote.

Are votive candles related to voting?

Etymologically, yes. Both words come from the Latin *votum*, meaning "vow."

What was the closest presidential race in U.S. history?

No, not the Bush-Gore scenario in 2000—it's much earlier. In the 1800 election, both Aaron Burr and Thomas Jefferson received 73 electoral votes. Members of the House of Representatives selected Jefferson as the winner.

Was that the only electoral vote tie in history?

Yes, but the 1824 election proved even more problematic. Andrew Jackson received more electoral votes (99) than John Quincy Adams (84), but neither had a majority, so again, the House of Representatives made the choice. They opted for Adams.

What American philosopher went to jail for not paying the poll tax?

Henry David Thoreau. He refused to contribute money that would be used to finance the Mexican War, and wrote the essay *Civil Disobedience* to explain his position.

Other than the fact that he was a comic-strip cat, what was unusual about Bill the Cat's entrance into the 1984 presidential race?

He was dead. And if there's anything weirder than a cartoon feline running for president, it's a dead cartoon feline running for president.

What new token was added to the Monopoly board game in a 1988 consumer vote?

A moneybag was the overwhelming choice, defeating the other options, a biplane and a piggy bank.

Taxes

Short supply led to the removal of the federal tax on what food item in 1950?

Margarine. A 10-cent-per-pound tax had been levied on margarine to protect dairy farmers from losing butter sales. A butter shortage finally forced Congress to repeal the tax.

Was the Boston Tea Party meant to protest British taxes on tea?

Only in a roundabout way. Actually, it was meant to protest His Majesty's removal of the tax. Americans had smuggled in Dutch tea to circumvent the high tariff on English tea, so King George reduced the tax, hoping to ruin the underground exchange.

What rocky period of U.S. history forced Congress to levy the first federal income tax?

The Civil War. The tax was first imposed in 1861, and outlived the War. It wasn't rescinded until 1872.

Spared prosecution for many heinous acts, what gangster was finally jailed for tax evasion in 1931?

Al Capone. He was found guilty and sentenced to 11 years in prison.

Who were the "Mr. Wilson" and "Mr. Heath" mentioned in the lyrics of The Beatles' 1966 song "Taxman"?

At the time, Harold Wilson was Labour Party leader and Prime Minister of Great Britain. Edward Heath was head of the Conservative Party and took over the PM job from Wilson in 1970.

What did England place a tax on in the eighteenth and early nineteenth centuries that changed the nation's architecture?

Windows. As a result, builders produced many structures with few (or no) windows.

Why did Congress tax whiskey so heavily in the 1790s?

Farmers were earning more by selling their grain to distillers than by selling it as food for the growing nation. They unsuccessfully attempted to fight back in what was called the Whiskey Rebellion.

What was the first state to impose a tax on gasoline?

Oregon, in 1919.

What states don't charge a sales tax on most purchases?

As of 2007, Alaska, Delaware, Montana, New Hampshire, and Oregon are the only states that do not charge a statewide sales tax.

Has "tax day" in the United States always been April 15?

Until 1955, federal income taxes were due on March 15. But as the middle class started paying more taxes, the IRS owed more refunds. The later date gave the government an extra month to hold on to our money.

How many tax returns are audited every year?

The number has increased. In 2000, just over 600,000 taxpayers were audited. In 2006, nearly 1.3 million folks were sent the dreaded notice.

Clothing

Who invented the brassiere?

New York socialite Mary Phelps Jacob. Unhappy with the way her corset poked out of her evening gown, she improvised a garment using a silk handkerchief and some pink ribbon. She patented the "backless brassiere" on November 3, 1914.

What does BVD stand for?

It's an acronym for Bradley, Voorhees, and Day, the last names of the three gentlemen who founded the clothing company in 1876.

Why is a man's formal suit called a tuxedo?

In the mid-1880s, James Potter started wearing a dinner jacket with satin lapels to formal events in New York's exclusive Tuxedo Park area. Once others copied his style, the name "tuxedo" stuck.

Who invented blue jeans?

During the California gold rush in 1853, dry-goods salesman Levi Strauss used twilled cotton fabric imported from France to make overalls with pockets for the treasure seekers. The fabric, serge de Nimes, later became known simply as "denim."

Who invented the zipper?

Gideon Sundback, an engineer at the Universal Fastener Company, took a crude design created by the company and turned it into the modern zipper (patented as the "Separable Fastener" in 1917).

Why do men's and women's shirts button on different sides?

Many believe that this tradition dates back to medieval times, when wealthy women were dressed by a nanny or maid. Men fastened their own shirts, while (usually right-handed) assistants buttoned up the ladies.

Why are surgical scrubs typically green?

In a surgical theater (where students observed procedures), the combination of bright lights and white scrubs caused too much glare. Tests revealed that a dull shade of green was easier on the eyes under those conditions.

When did pantyhose enter the marketplace?

Even after nylon stockings were invented, women still needed garter belts to hold them in place. In 1959, Allen Gant Sr. of North Carolina's Glen Raven Mills introduced the one-piece nylon garment now known as pantyhose.

Which came first—boxers or briefs?

Boxer shorts, by about a decade. Jacob Golomb, founder of the Everlast Company, introduced elastic-waist boxers in 1925. Arthur Kneibler patented the Jockey brief in 1934.

How did T-shirts get their name?

They were actually originally called "gob shirts" back in 1938, but once they gained popularity during World War II, the shirts became known as T-shirts after the shape they made when spread out flat.

Schools and Learning

Why are first-year students called "freshmen," and second-year students "sophomores"?

At Cambridge University in the sixteenth century, a first-year student was called a fresh-man, while other students were called junior sophists and senior sophists (sophist meaning "wise man"). The founder of Harvard University used variations of this British terminology for his new four-year school.

Which eight universities make up the Ivy League?

Brown, Columbia, Cornell, Dartmouth, Harvard, Penn, Princeton, and Yale.

Which colleges comprise the Seven Sisters (the feminine counterpart to the Ivy League)?

Actually, only five "sisters" remain, because Radcliffe merged with Harvard and Vassar became coeducational. The others are Barnard, Bryn Mawr, Mount Holyoke, Smith, and Wellesley.

Has the school year always run from September to June?

No. During the 1800s, farm children attended school twice a year, from December to March, and again from mid-May to August. The rest of the time, they were helping with planting or harvesting. Urban children of that era typically observed an 11-month school year.

Why are school buses yellow?

To make them more visible to drivers. The color is actually a yellow-orange blend, which, after much testing, was determined to be the easiest color for the human eye to detect under various lighting and weather conditions.

Why aren't school buses equipped with seat belts?

School-bus seats are specially designed in a "compartment" fashion—high-backed and well-padded—in order to absorb crash forces. Seat belts could be a hindrance in a panic situation, with one driver frantically trying to unbuckle a busload of frightened children.

Why were few early American teachers married?

Until the turn of the twentieth century, a teacher had to relinquish her job if she became wed. The logic was that a married woman had a husband to support her and had no need to take a "woman's job" away from a needy spinster.

Why is the first year of school called "kindergarten"?

Friedrich Froebel, a German teacher who created the concept of a class where children would learn socialization skills via play, called his class kindergarten. It's a German term meaning "children's garden."

Who wrote the popular **Dick and Jane** *primary reader books?*

William Gray, Sterl Artley, and May Hill Arbuthnot were the authors. By the early 1960s, it was estimated that 85 percent of American school children learned to read via the series' stories.

Why is a diploma sometimes called a "sheepskin"?

In the days before paper was practical to produce, the skins of animals (usually sheep) were the preferred medium for handwritten diplomas.

Medications

When were childproof caps on medicine containers introduced?

The "palm-and-twist" cap was invented in 1967 by a Canadian pediatrician named Henri Breault. In the United States, they became required by law in 1972.

Why do pills come in so many different shapes and colors?

It's a way to help the visually impaired to differentiate between their medications. The colors also serve as a quick visual ID for caregivers who dispense the same pills to patients on a regular basis.

Why is "R$_x$" an abbreviation for "prescription"?

It's actually not "R$_x$" but an R with a line crossing its tail. It stands for the Latin word *recipere*, which means "to take."

What was the first medicine sold in pill form?

Aspirin. Salicylic acid had been used as an analgesic since the early nineteenth century, but it wasn't until Bayer developed a water-soluble tablet in 1899 that folks could take it without it irritating their stomachs.

Speaking of Bayer, didn't they once sell heroin over the counter?

Yep. In 1874, Bayer researchers developed a formula for a painkiller they thought might be less addictive than morphine. They called it heroin, from the German word heroisch, meaning "heroic." They sold it as a cough medicine until 1910.

Why are prescription medications so expensive?

By the time a drug finally makes it all the way to the FDA for approval, the pharmaceutical company has already spent (on average) 15 years and $500 million developing and testing it. And for about every 5,000 compounds that make it to the testing stage, only one will be approved.

How was it discovered that nitroglycerin eased the pain of heart disease?

During the 1860s, workers at Alfred Nobel's dynamite factory who suffered from heart conditions noticed that (opposite to most of us) their chest pains eased once they came to work. It was eventually discovered that nitroglycerin dilates the blood vessels, which provided relief from clogged arteries.

How does aspirin help during a heart attack?

It prevents blood platelets from sticking to one another and forming a clot, which is one of the triggering factors in a heart attack. Doctors recommend chewing rather than swallowing the aspirin.

How was the, er, "staying power" of Viagra discovered?

Sildenafil citrate (Viagra) was originally tested as a treatment for high blood pressure. But when the clinical trials ended, and the majority of the male subjects refused to return their unused pills, Pfizer suspected something was up (no pun intended).

Is my bathroom medicine cabinet the best place to store my prescriptions?

No. Moisture breaks down medications, and the humidity after you shower seeps into the medicine cabinet.

Children and Parents

How many siblings are there in the musical Jackson family (including Michael)?

Nine: Janet, Jermaine, LaToya, Marlon, Maureen (Rebbie), Michael, Sigmund (Jackie), Steven (Randy), and Toriano (Tito).

Do girls stop growing quicker than boys?

When it comes to height, yes. The average American boy and girl both grow at a steady rate to an average of 5'2" at age 13. From there, females tend to stop growing taller, while males may continue to get taller for another five years, or even longer.

How many children are born to single parents?

In the United States, single parents represent 27 percent of the households with children under the age of 18. The number of babies born to unmarried women increased from 3 million in 1970 to 10 million in 2000.

What is an "emancipated minor"?

In the United States, a person is considered legally free of parental control at the age of 18. However, anyone 14 or older can petition the court to be considered an adult by proving financial support or security.

What's the difference between a half-sibling and a step-sibling?

A half-sibling is a child of one of your parents and another person. A step-sibling is an existing child of someone who marries one of your parents (but is not biologically related to you or your parent).

On what sitcom did a man named Robert play a character named Michael, and a boy named Michael play his son, a character named Robert?

The Brady Bunch. Robert Reed was Mike Brady, while Mike Lookinland portrayed his son, Bobby Brady.

The human family in what comic strip consists of parents Dottie and Phil and children Barbara and Billy?

Marmaduke.

What unlikely pair portrayed Chandler Bing's parents on the hit sitcom Friends?

Morgan Fairchild played his mother Nora, while Kathleen Turner used her resonant voice to great effect as his drag-queen father, Charles.

*What do TV characters Ernie Douglas (*My Three Sons*), Bamm-Bamm Rubble (*The Flintstones*), and Webster Long (*Webster*) have in common?*

They were each adopted.

And speaking of Webster, what was unusual about the parents who adopted him (other than being of a different race)?

The couple who portrayed his adoptive parents—Alex Karras and Susan Clark—are married in real life.

How many children did Jed Clampett have on The Beverly Hillbillies?

Only one, Elly May. Jethro Bodine was Jed's nephew.

In his 1979 Oscar acceptance speech, what actor thanked his parents "for not practicing birth control"?

Dustin Hoffman.

How many children are there in the average U.S. family?

In the early 1800s, the average couple produced seven children. By the early 1900s, that number had decreased to four. Since 1960, the number has remained steady at an average of two children per family.

Jobs and Working

Recent U.S. studies have revealed what job as being the most dangerous?

Timber cutting, with a fatality rate 50 percent higher than the next-most-dangerous job, commercial fishing.

What is widely promoted as "the toughest job you'll ever love"?

The Peace Corps.

What superheroine started out as a military secretary, but (in a later version of her comic book) went on to a less-stellar job at a Taco Whiz restaurant?

Diana Prince (a.k.a. Wonder Woman).

How did Dick Clark get the job hosting TV's American Bandstand?

The show's original host, Bob Horn, was arrested for drunk driving. This happened to occur in the midst of a safe-driver campaign by Philadelphia's WFIL-TV, so Horn was fired and Clark took over the spot.

What small item of office equipment was made famous by the film Office Space?

The red Swingline stapler. The company had never produced their signature stapler in red—the one in the film had been specially painted. After the movie became a cult hit, Swingline offered a special limited edition in red.

What state has the highest percentage of union workers?

Hawaii, with a full 25 percent of its wage and salary workers belonging to a labor organization.

And which state has the lowest?

South Carolina, with only 2 percent.

What company employed Scott Adams through 1995, giving him plenty of fodder for his Dilbert *comic strip?*

Pacific Bell.

What name was shared by the telephone operator on the sitcoms Green Acres, Petticoat Junction, *and* The Andy Griffith Show?

Sarah.

What is a desairologist?

A licensed cosmetologist who specializes in styling the hair of the deceased for funeral directors.

What type of farmers lobbied the loudest against the implementation of Daylight Savings Time?

Dairy farmers. It's difficult and uncomfortable for the cows to change their daily milking times, even to accommodate schedules for production (creameries) and transportation (railroads).

When did the United States first establish a minimum wage?

Franklin D. Roosevelt signed into law America's first minimum wage on June 25, 1938, ensuring that every U.S. worker would earn at least 25 cents per hour.

Sleeping

Does the body really have an "internal" alarm clock?

Yes. When the brain has become accustomed to a regular routine, it will send signals to the body to "wake up" even when another stimulus (in this case, usually an alarm clock) fails.

What story character slept in the woods for 100 years?

None that we know of. Rip Van Winkle only slept for 20 years. In the original tale, he slept right through the American Revolution.

Does "counting sheep" help you to fall asleep?

No. Researchers have found that visualizing tranquil scenery is the best way to prepare for sleep.

Why do many sleepers subconsciously flip over their pillows while sleeping?

It's a natural way of trying to keep cool and comfortable. Most of the body's heat is dispersed through the head, and this warms up the pillow after a period of time.

Is it dangerous to wake up someone who is sleepwalking?

Only if the snoozer is in a precarious position to begin with. In fact, it often ends up being worse for the "waker" than for the "wakee," as sleepwalkers may flail their arms or legs while waking up.

Why do circles form under the eyes when we get drowsy?

As the human body tires, blood circulation slows down to conserve energy. The skin becomes paler, and the thin skin under the eyes is one of the first spots where tiny, dark blood vessels begin to show through.

On the same note, why do bags form under the eyes of some sleepers?

Bodily fluids tend to pool in the orbital cavities surrounding the eyes, causing the condition. After a short period of time in an upright position, the bags often dissipate.

What happens if you tear off the "Do Not Remove Under Penalty of Law" tag on your mattress?

Nothing. The tags simply describe the composition of the mattress to help determine if a potential buyer might be allergic to the material. But the label is meant for retailers, not consumers.

Do dog and cat owners typically sleep with their pets?

More than one third of dog owners do. For cat owners, a full two thirds bed down with their feline. Or, more accurately, two thirds of felines choose to sleep with their owners.

Waterbeds became popular in the 1970s. Why did no one come up with the idea before that?

Actually, enclosed waterbeds date to at least a century earlier, when they were used to help alleviate the aching joints and bedsores suffered by bedridden patients. They didn't succeed in the consumer market until a practical way was found to heat the beds and make them comfortable for everyday use.

Fashion, Styles, and Trends

Was Bo Derek the first media star to sport cornrows in her hair?

Not by a long shot. Back in 1963, Cicely Tyson wore the style when she appeared as secretary Jane Foster in the short-lived Emmy-winning drama *East Side/West Side.* (The star? George C. Scott.)

Who invented the mini-skirt?

There is some debate over who came up with the original concept, but London fashion designer Mary Quant is known for having made it a fashion statement in the early 1960s.

What was the first printed T-shirt design to sell over a million garments?

The one featuring Farrah Fawcett's famous swimsuit pose, licensed by a company called Factors in 1976.

What company started the designer jeans craze?

The Nakash brothers of New York City manufactured their own line of tight-fitting, dark-washed jeans with a prominent logo on the back pocket in 1978. They called their company Jordache, and soon, other designers started producing high-end denim trousers.

What Saturday Night Live *actors popularized the following once-trendy phrases?*

1. *"Not!"*
   Mike Myers

2. *"That's the ticket!"*
   Jon Lovitz

3. *"Buh-bye!"*
   David Spade

4. *"Well, isn't that special?"*
   Dana Carvey

5. *"Never mind."*
   Gilda Radner

6. *"You look marvelous!"*
   Billy Crystal

How did wearing pants below the belt line become fashionable?

The trend, called "sagging," originated in the prison system. Belts are taken away before prisoners are locked up, allowing gravity to work its magic.

How did the heavy-metal hair bands get their hair to stand up in huge haystacks?

No fancy-schmancy designer products were involved. Members of groups from Mötley Crüe to Poison to Ratt have divulged the same secret to their gravity-defying hair: Aqua Net hairspray.

Where and when did the wet T-shirt contest originate?

At an Idaho ski lodge in January 1971. A company called K2 was handing out dozens of promotional T-shirts during a convention of flight attendants, and the combination of an indoor pool and lots of booze spawned the first such event.

What inspired the "torn sweats" look in the film Flashdance?

The film's producers noted that professional dancers often wore sweatshirts during warm-up exercises in order to keep their chest/lungs warm in cold dance studios, but that they preferred to cut the sleeves off for freedom of movement.

What Woody Allen film launched a popular fashion trend?

In 1977's *Annie Hall*, Diane Keaton was featured in a variety of men's rumpled clothes—baggy trousers, neckties, oversized vests, and slouchy jackets. Fashionistas note that the film popularized the androgynous look.

SPORTS 3

Baseball

Who invented baseball?

No one, really. It evolved over time from a few similar games that had been played for centuries. What we do know is that most of the basic rules of today were standard by the 1850s, and that the story of Abner Doubleday's role in the "invention" of the sport is a myth.

What are the guidelines for the dimensions of an outfield in a major league ballpark?

Previously, MLB rules only mandated that the nearest outfield fence be no less than 250 feet from home plate. In 1958, the rules were changed for all new professional stadiums, requiring a distance of at least 325 feet along the foul lines and no less than 400 feet to center field.

How is slugging average different from batting average?

Instead of dividing at-bats by hits, the slugging average divides total bases by hits. It's a way to distinguish "power hitters" from the rest of the pack. Players who hit more doubles, triples, and home runs will have a much higher slugging average.

Why is home plate five-sided while all the other bases are square?

The flat area facing the pitcher's mound helps make the strike zone more visual, proving beneficial for batters, pitchers, and umpires.

What 2003 MLB rule change gave the annual All-Star Game more significance?

The winning league is awarded home-field advantage in that season's World Series.

Why do official scorers use the letter "K" instead of "S" to indicate a strikeout?

Early newspaper journalists who reported on games didn't want to miss any of the action while buried in a notebook, so they developed a quick way of indicating what each player did. They couldn't use "S" (sacrifice) or "SO" ("shutout"), so they took the last letter of "struck" (as in "struck out") instead.

Why is this "K" sometimes written backward?

It's a quick way for scorers to distinguish how a batter struck out. A "swinging" strikeout is indicated by a regular "K," and the letter is written backward if the batter struck out "looking" (without swinging at the third strike).

In 2004, Barry Bonds broke the single-season record for most what?

No, it wasn't home runs (he broke that record in 2007). It was for bases-on-balls. His 232 that year set a new record and also gave him the career record (2,190) that had been previously held by Rickey Henderson.

What key element is missing from Major League Baseball salaries when compared to those in the NFL, NBA, and NHL?

Pro baseball teams have no salary cap. In the other sports, each team is allotted a maximum amount of money annually to spend on players, resulting in a better balance of talent across the league. To date, MLB hasn't adopted such a limitation.

What happens when an MLB player loses his jersey?

Pro teams typically have spares on hand, but by rule, "No player whose uniform does not conform to that of his teammates shall be permitted to participate in a game."

What's the key rule difference in the National League and American League?

It all comes down to a single, controversial decision made in 1970: the adoption of the Designated Hitter. In order to "liven up" the sport, the AL changed the rules to allow a player of choice to bat in the pitcher's spot, which they believed made the matchups more entertaining for fans. The NL still requires its pitchers to take their own turns at bat.

Basketball

Why are basketball players called "cagers"?

In the early days of the game, the rules stated that an out-of-bounds ball belonged to the first team to touch it after it crossed the line. Arenas started building chicken-wire enclosures around the court in order to protect the crowd from errant balls and stampeding players.

Why did the 1971 and 1972 NBA Most Valuable Player awards show different names, when they were given to the same player?

When said MVP led the Milwaukee Bucks to the NBA title in 1971, he was known as Lew Alcindor. He adopted a Muslim name in the off-season, so the following year's trophy was inscribed Kareem Abdul-Jabbar.

What's the only Division I college basketball team to have an all-time winning percentage of more than .750?

The University of Kentucky Wildcats. If they continue their success, they should become the first team to win 2,000 games.

Who holds the NBA record for highest career scoring average?

It's Michael Jordan, but only by a fraction. He scored 30.12 points per game, while Wilt Chamberlain could muster only 30.07.

In 2006, what men's college basketball team became the first in more than 60 years to repeat as NIT champions?

South Carolina. The reason it's such a difficult feat is that a team has to be "average" enough to fail to earn an NCAA tournament berth, but "good" enough to defeat all the other teams in the NIT.

Who was the first NBA player to shatter a backboard?

Chuck Connors of the Boston Celtics broke the backboard while warming up at Boston Arena on November 5, 1946. (Yes, the same Chuck Connors who starred on TV's *The Rifleman*.)

Weren't there red, white, and blue basketballs at one time?

Yes. Spalding made them for the American Basketball Association from 1967 to 1976, and the Harlem Globetrotters used them as well.

Speaking of the Harlem Globetrotters, have any of the team's members gone on to play in the NBA?

Yes. When the NBA lifted the "whites only" rule in 1950, teams immediately began poaching players from the Globetrotters, including a young Wilt Chamberlain.

Why are basketball shorts so long in today's game?

The style apparently came about after Michael Jordan developed the habit of bending over to catch his breath. He'd hold on to the legs of his shorts for support, causing the fabric to stretch. Soon, everyone wanted "long" shorts like His Airness.

Who was the first college player to slam-dunk a basketball?

Bob Kurland, a 7-foot-tall center for Oklahoma A&M from 1942 to 1946, was the first player to regularly dunk during games. Other players had done it during practice, but because it was considered "showboating," they'd refrained from dunking during games.

Football

What three current NFL franchises began life in Cleveland, Ohio?

◆ Baltimore Ravens (Cleveland Browns, 1946)

◆ St. Louis Rams (Cleveland Rams, 1936)

◆ Cleveland Browns (Cleveland Browns, 1996)

What position was played by all of the top-10 leading NFL lifetime scorers?

Placekicker. Because kickers earn field-goal opportunities when the offense can't otherwise score (and because they kick extra points after most TDs, no matter who scored them), they usually contribute more points than any other player.

What college football team has "shared" the national championship three times since 1974?

The University of Southern California. The two national polls can't always agree on a champion, so the Trojans had to split the honors with Oklahoma (1974), Alabama (1978), and LSU (2003). The team finally won a consensus championship in 2004.

What Southeastern Conference football team has been involved in two seven-overtime games (an NCAA record)?

The University of Arkansas Razorbacks. They won both games (58–56 over Mississippi in 2001, and 71–63 over Kentucky in 2003).

In what city did these current NFL teams originate?

1. *Arizona Cardinals?*
   Chicago.

2. *Chicago Bears?*
   Decatur, Illinois.

3. *Detroit Lions?*
   Portsmouth, Ohio.

4. *Indianapolis Colts?*
   Baltimore.

5. *Kansas City Chiefs?*
   Dallas.

6. *San Diego Chargers?*
   Los Angeles.

7. *Tennessee Titans?*
   Houston.

8. *Washington Redskins?*
   Boston.

What stadium hosted three of the first five Super Bowl games?

The Orange Bowl in Miami. Super Bowls II, III, and V were played there (along with X and XIII).

Running back Mike Hart of the University of Michigan carried the ball 993 consecutive times without doing what?

Losing a fumble. In his final game, Michigan beat Florida in the Capital One Bowl on New Year's Day 2008. Hart lost *two* fumbles in the matchup, but also scored two TDs to lead the Wolverines to victory.

What three teams from the old All-America Football Conference (AAFC) joined the NFL in 1950?

The Baltimore Colts, Cleveland Browns, and San Francisco 49ers.

What three NFL teams joined the American Football Conference when the league merged with the AFL in 1970?

The Baltimore Colts, Cleveland Browns, and Pittsburgh Steelers.

Ice Hockey

Who was the first NHL player to score 1,000 goals?

Gordie Howe hit this landmark on November 27, 1960.

The home ice of what NHL team is located in the oldest (and smallest) arena in the league?

The New York Islanders. They play their games at Nassau Veterans Memorial Coliseum, built in 1972, with a capacity of just over 16,000.

Why are three goals in a game called a "hat trick"?

The term originated in the English game of cricket, where any player who took three wickets was awarded a new hat. During the 1940s, a Toronto, Ontario, haberdasher continued the tradition by giving a free hat to any Maple Leaf who scored three goals.

Who was the first goaltender to employ a facemask during an official game?

Jacques Plante of the Montreal Canadiens broke with tradition in 1959 when he insisted on wearing his protective practice mask during the game. At the time, he had 200 fresh stitches in his face from a previous slap shot.

Which NHL player was the first to use a curved blade?

Andy Bathgate of the New York Rangers. In the late 1950s, he used to soak his blades in hot water and then bend them in the door jambs of the restroom stalls.

Can you identify these annual NHL awards?

1. *The Hart Memorial Trophy?*
   Most Valuable Player in the league.

2. *The Conn Smythe Trophy?*
   Most Valuable Player in the playoffs.

3. *The Calder Memorial Trophy?*
   Rookie of the Year.

4. *The Lady Byng Memorial Trophy?*
   Most Gentlemanly Player.

5. *The James Norris Memorial Trophy?*
   Outstanding Defenseman.

6. *The Art Ross Trophy?*
   Leading Points Scorer.

7. *The Vezina Trophy?*
   Outstanding Goalie.

Why did Wayne Gretzky always tuck in only one side of his jersey?

When the Great One was just five years old, he was already competing against kids twice his age. His ill-fitting jersey was much too large for him, so his father used to tuck it in on the boy's shooting side to prevent it from getting in his way. Gretzky continued this tradition as a tribute to his dad and a "good luck" omen.

Who invented the Zamboni?

Not surprising, a gentleman named Frank Zamboni. He was a mechanic in the refrigeration business, and when he noted in the late 1930s that it took a crew of four men an hour to resurface the local ice skating rink, he applied his knowledge and used an old tractor to build his first Zamboni.

Why does the Zamboni have headlights?

Quite often, the vehicle must leave the arena and drive in the dark to dump snow into a collection tank.

Tennis

Why is a zero score in tennis referred to as "love"?

It was adapted from the phrase "to play for the love of the game," or to play without any sort of wager, for nothing. The old theory that the term came from *l'oeuf*, the French word for "egg" (which is shaped like a zero), is just a legend.

Why is the word "seed" used when ranking players?

In 1898, the American Lawn Tennis Association decided that the best players should be "scattered like seed" through the championship draw so that they'd be separated far from one another.

What player is responsible for changing the dress code in professional tennis?

The All-England Lawn Tennis and Croquet Club, a.k.a. Wimbledon, had a very strict dress code for players. When American tennis star Gertrude Moran showed up in 1949 wearing a short skirt with ruffled, lace-trimmed knickers peeking out from underneath, she caused a sensation. When Wimbledon saw the enormous (and positive) press coverage Moran received, they relaxed their uniform rules.

How did the Davis Cup get its name?

The premiere event in men's professional tennis was conceived in 1899 by members of the Harvard University tennis team. One of those players was Dwight Filley Davis, who reached into his own pocket to pay for the sterling silver trophy that would be presented to the winner.

What's the difference in the style of play between a clay court, a hard court, and a grass court?

Clay courts are made of crushed shale or stone and are considered slow—balls have less bounce and forward motion. Hard courts are made of cement or plastic and are faster than clay courts. Grass makes for the fastest court; the surface is less firm and more slippery than hard courts, forcing players to race to the ball more quickly.

Why are tennis balls fuzzy?

The "fuzz" (made of wool and officially called *felt*) on tennis balls helps players to control their shots. It creates friction and makes topspin and backspin more pronounced.

Why was the standard color for tennis balls changed from white to fluorescent yellow?

That color is officially called "optic yellow" and is considered to have the best overall visibility. Orange was experimented with at one time, but it did not show up on television as well as optic yellow.

Who popularized tennis bracelets?

During a game in 1987, Chris Evert asked officials to temporarily halt the competition after the clasp on her channel-set diamond bracelet broke. Her jewelry was recovered, the game resumed, and similar accessories have been called "tennis bracelets" ever since.

What are the strings in tennis racquets made of?

Even though natural strings are often referred to as "catgut," they were made from the intestines of cows, not cats. However, only a few elite professional players use natural gut today; most players prefer synthetic strings.

Is tennis a sport at the Olympic Games?

Now, yes. The sport was dropped from the games in 1924, but made a comeback at the 1988 games in Seoul.

Golf

Why are most golf courses 9 or 18 holes long?

It was a standard set by the world's most famous golf course, St. Andrew's in Scotland, which was redesigned in 1858 to accommodate 18 holes (two on each of the nine greens).

What's the real first name of golf phenom Tiger Woods?

Eldrick.

What former TV talk-show host swung an imaginary golf club during each show?

Johnny Carson of *The Tonight Show.*

How did the term "bogey" originate?

From British golfers who blamed the "Bogey Man" for their poor play.

Why are golfers permitted to only carry 14 clubs at a time?

For the same reason that three strikes is an out in baseball, and you must get 10 yards for a first down in football: those are the rules!

Why is Jack Nicklaus called the "Golden Bear"?

Because he played golf for Upper Arlington High School in suburban Columbus, Ohio; the school's sports teams are known as the Golden Bears.

Who turned down the title role on TV's Columbo because he said it would interfere with his golf?

Bing Crosby. The role went to Peter Falk instead.

Is the word "golf" an acronym for "Gentlemen Only, Ladies Forbidden"?

No. It's thought to have been derived from an old Dutch word that means "club."

The Olympic Games

What was the only competition during the first recorded Olympics, held in 776 B.C.E. in Greece?

The 200-yard dash.

What are the colors of the five rings in the Olympic logo?

Black, blue, green, red, and yellow.

What two martial arts are included in the Summer Olympic Games?

Judo (since 1964) and Tae kwon do (since 2000).

What tennis star's father was a boxer for the U.S. Olympic Team?

Andre Agassi.

What 1972 Olympic athlete raised eyebrows by posing nude in an issue of Sports Illustrated?

Cathy Rigby.

What former Olympic star took over for Erik Estrada on TV's CHiPs *during a short-lived salary dispute?*

Bruce Jenner.

Oscar-winner Geena Davis trained in what sport, reaching the semifinals but failing to become part of the 1996 U.S. Olympic team?

Archery.

What first name was shared by two members of the 1996 gold-medal-winning U.S. Women's Gymnastics team?

Dominique (Dawes and Moceanu).

What U.S. city was initially awarded the Winter Olympic Games in 1976?

Denver, Colorado. Voters refused to pass taxes to finance the necessary facilities, however, so the event moved to Innsbruck, Austria.

What nation did the U.S. Hockey Team defeat in 1980 to win the gold medal?

Finland. (The famous "Miracle on Ice" game with the USSR was a semi-final game.)

What was the last year during which both the Summer and Winter Olympics were held?

1992.

Racing

Which racing cars have the fastest "flat-out" top speed: NASCAR cars, Formula One cars, or Top Fuel Dragster cars?

Dragsters, which can exceed 325 mph. Formula One cars would max out at around 250 mph, while uninhibited NASCAR vehicles might reach 225 mph.

Who was the first driver to win NASCAR's Winston Cup (now known as the Nextel Cup) for three consecutive years?

Cale Yarborough, in 1976, 1977, and 1978.

What else did Cale Yarborough accomplish in 1977 that had never been done before in NASCAR history?

He started—and more important, finished—every race on the schedule that season.

Toyota Camrys were introduced to the NASCAR Nextel Cup in 2007; are they the first foreign cars to appear on that circuit?

No. British-built Jaguars were raced in NASCAR back in the 1950s.

And what's ironic about the entry of those Toyotas into NASCAR?

They were the only U.S. built cars to compete in the Nextel Cup in 2007. Toyota Camrys are built in Kentucky, whereas the for-sale versions of the Chevrolet, Ford, and Dodge models that compete are built in Canada or Mexico.

In what famous race did the biggest pileup in NASCAR history occur back in 1960?

The Daytona 500. More than half the cars in the field (37 of 68) were involved in the wreck.

What popular brand name has sponsored the NASCAR Truck Series since 1995?

Craftsman.

What driver came from the last position to nearly win the 1992 Indy 500?

Scott Goodyear. The Canadian driver never led the race but nearly took it at the end, falling to Al Unser Jr. by only 0.045 seconds.

What 1912 invention by O. P. Smith revolutionized greyhound racing?

The mechanical rabbit. Prior to that time, a real rabbit was chased (and often caught) by the speedy dogs.

Why are quarter horses named so?

Because they typically run races of one quarter of a mile in length.

College Sports

John Heisman, for whom the Heisman Trophy is named, played his college football at what southern university?

Georgia Tech.

Former University of Louisville basketball player Derek Smith claims to have invented what now-common celebratory maneuver?

The high-five.

What film character played football for the fictional South Central Louisiana State University Mud Dogs?

Bobby Boucher, *The Waterboy.*

What school dominated NCAA wrestling from 1975–2000, winning 20 national championships in that span?

The University of Iowa.

Per NCAA rules, how many hours per week are college students allowed to spend performing "athletic-related activities" during the season?

Twenty. Those 20 hours must be in increments of fewer than four hours a day. Off-season, the limit is only eight hours per week.

What are college baseball players allowed to use while at the plate that professional ones are not?

An aluminum bat.

Was Gatorade really named because it was first made at the University of Florida?

Yes. Researchers developed the beverage to help football players replenish fluids lost while playing in the sweltering Florida heat.

What's the only university to feature a Walt Disney character as its sports mascot?

The University of Oregon Ducks.

Gymnastics and Skating

Why do the jumps in figure skating have such funny names?

They're named after the athletes (such as Ulrich *Salchow* and Alois *Lutz*) who first performed them in competition and are considered the "inventors" of the move.

Who started the tradition of short skirts for female figure skaters?

Sonja Henie revolutionized figure skating in the early 1900s by wearing short, fur-trimmed white skirts (instead of the traditional long black). Henie won a total of 10 world championships and three Olympic gold medals during her career.

After the Nancy Kerrigan/Tanya Harding scandal, how did the two finally place at the 1994 Winter Olympics?

Despite an impressive program, Kerrigan won the silver medal, losing the gold to Russia's Oksana Baiul by one tenth of a point. Harding ended up in eighth place.

Can anyone with enough talent become an elite figure skater?

Not without a wealthy sponsor. The cost of private lessons, ice time, custom-made boots, blades, and specially designed costumes runs an average of about $130,000 per year.

Was Olga Korbut the first gymnast to perform an aerial back somersault on the balance beam?

No. Even though every 1972 Olympic film montage shows Korbut's famous salto, Nancy Thies of the United States performed the same move at the same Olympic Games seven hours earlier.

Who was the first gymnast to score a perfect 10 at the Olympics?

Nadia Comaneci was the first. The Romanian racked up seven 10s in 1976, and Russian gymnast Nelli Kim also received two perfect scores that year. The code of points has since been modified, so a 10 is much more difficult to achieve.

What is the difference between artistic gymnastics and rhythmic gymnastics?

Artistic gymnastics consists of the floor, beam, bars, and vault events. Rhythmic gymnastics is a combination of dance and acrobatics performed on the floor while using balls, hoops, ribbons, ropes, and clubs as "props."

What is the Olympic order of events for gymnastics?

For men:

♦ Floor exercise

♦ Pommel horse

♦ Still rings

♦ Vault

♦ Parallel bars

♦ Horizontal bar

For women:

♦ Vault

♦ Uneven bars

♦ Balance beam

♦ Floor exercise

Why are female gymnasts typically so young, while the men are college-aged?

Women's gymnastics requires a light, flexible body with a low center of gravity, which is generally found in prepubescent girls. Men's events rely on upper-body strength, which men don't develop properly until their late teens.

PEOPLE and NAMES

Pseudonyms

Was Marilyn Monroe's real last name Baker?

No, not legally. Her birth certificate said Norma Jeane Mortenson, and her father was listed as Martin Edward Mortensen. But because Marilyn's mother (Gladys Baker) wasn't convinced that Mortensen was the real father, she had the young girl baptized with her own last name.

What does the "G" stand for in the name of musician Kenny G?

Gorelick, his last name.

Why did Stan Laurel (of Laurel and Hardy fame) change his name?

Arthur Stanley Jefferson was content to be known as Stan Jefferson until a vaudeville partner pointed out to him that the name had 13 letters, which might hinder his success. She suggested that he adopt the surname Laurel.

What's John Wayne's real name?

He was born Marion Morrison, but his middle name is tough to pin down. His parents said it was Mitchell, and he said it was Michael, but his birth certificate indicated it was Robert.

Is there a real person behind the name Alan Smithee that appears in film credits so often?

No. Since at least 1968, it's been used as the pseudonym of various film directors who decided at the completion of a project that they no longer wanted credit for it.

Who is Richard Bachman?

You'd recognize him as Stephen King. Richard Bachman is a pen-name King used for several novels that didn't match his normal style of writing.

Why do experts recommend you use a pseudonym when blogging?

Blogs are online diaries, and many folks like to reveal shady goings-on at their jobs or even illegal activities in which they participate. Many employers now regularly Google names, as does the FBI, so it's best to remain anonymous if you're going to bare your soul online.

Was novelist George Eliot really a woman?

Yes. Mary Ann Evans wrote under a male pseudonym to ensure that her works (such as *Silas Marner*) would be taken seriously.

Why did members of the punk rock band The Ramones adopt that as their surname?

They were inspired by Paul McCartney, who revealed that he'd used Paul Ramon as a pseudonym (before The Beatles became famous) because he thought it sounded exotic.

One-Named People

These celebrities are known by one name, but is it part of their real name?

- ◆ *Anastacia?*
  Yes (Anastacia Newkirk).

- ◆ *Bono?*
  No (Paul Hewson).

- ◆ *Brandy?*
  Yes (Brandy Norwood).

- ◆ *Charo?*
  No (Maria Baeza).

- ◆ *Cher?*
  Yes (Cherilyn Sarkisian LaPierre).

- *Dion?*
  Yes (Dion DiMucci).

- *Divine?*
  No (Harris Glenn Milstead).

- *Eve?*
  Yes (Eve Jeffers).

- *Fabio?*
  Yes (Fabio Lanzoni).

- *Jewel?*
  Yes (Jewel Kilcher).

- *Liberace?*
  Yes (Wladziu Liberace).

- *Nas?*
  Yes (Nasir bin Olu Dara Jones).

- *Pelé?*
  No (Edson Arantes do Nascimento).

- *Prince?*
  Yes (Prince Nelson).

- *Sade?*
  No (Helen Adu).

- *Seal?*
  Yes (Sealhenry Samuel).

- *Sinbad?*
  No (David Adkins).

- *Sisqó?*
  No (Mark Andrews).

◆ *Sting?*
No (Gordon Sumner is the singer; Steve Borden is the wrestler).

◆ *Tiffany?*
Yes (Tiffany Darwish).

◆ *Twiggy?*
No (Leslie Hornby).

◆ *Usher?*
Yes (Usher Raymond IV).

◆ *Yanni?*
Yes (Yanni Chrysomallis).

Named After

Who are the Teenage Mutant Ninja Turtles named after?

Some very famous Renaissance artists—Leonardo da Vinci, Donatello (Donato di Niccolo di Betto Bardi), Michelangelo Buonarroti, and Raphael Sanzio.

America is named after the explorer Amerigo Vespucci; why isn't it called Vespucciland?

In his lifetime, Vespucci was better known by his first name. Also, early mapmakers thought that America (beginning and ending with an A) sounded better alongside names like Africa and Asia.

How did the Jeep get its name?

Based on interviews with those who helped develop the vehicle, it was named after a creature in the *Popeye* comic strip called Eugene the Jeep. Jeeps could walk up walls, solve complex problems, and cross over into the fourth dimension.

Were Fig Newtons named after Sir Isaac Newton?

Nabisco's tradition in the early days of the company was to name its products after nearby communities. Fig Newtons are named after Newton, Massachusetts.

As of 2007, what three Star Trek principals each have an asteroid named for them?

George Takei (Lt. Sulu) with 7307 Takei, Nichelle Nichols (Lt. Uhura) with 68410 Nichols, and series creator Gene Roddenberry with 4659 Roddenberry. These were registered and approved by the International Astronomical Union (IAU).

On that note, can I really name a star after someone if I pay a fee?

No. Those ads promise to "register" a star in your name, which simply means they'll record it in a book or database. It has no scientific validity. Only the IAU has the authority to name celestial bodies, and they call star registry schemes a "deplorable commercial trick."

Why do we call a dance where the women invite the men a "Sadie Hawkins" dance?

The tradition was named after a character in the comic strip *Li'l Abner*. Sadie Hawkins was the ugliest girl in Dogpatch, and her father summoned all of the bachelors in the area and told them to start running when he fired his gun, because the man Sadie caught would become her husband.

How many of his children did George Foreman name after himself?

The heavyweight champion has 10 children; all five of his sons are named George, one of his daughters is Georgette, and another is Freda George.

Why was Cape Canaveral changed to Cape Kennedy and then changed back to Cape Canaveral?

President Kennedy was a space enthusiast, so after his death, widow Jackie suggested naming the NASA launch center in Florida after him. President Johnson proceeded to also rename the land that housed the center. Local Floridians objected to that change, however, and the cape itself was re-rechristened Canaveral in 1973.

Siblings

Are these celebrities siblings, or are they not related?

◆ *Julia Duffy and Patrick Duffy?*
Not related.

◆ *Faith Ford and Harrison Ford?*
Not related.

◆ *Jake Gyllenhaal and Maggie Gyllenhaal?*
Siblings.

◆ *Diane Keaton and Michael Keaton?*
Not related.

◆ *Dudley Moore and Roger Moore?*
Not related.

◆ *Bill Murray and Brian Doyle-Murray?*
Siblings.

◆ *Dennis Quaid and Randy Quaid?*
Siblings.

◆ *Rex Reed and Robert Reed?*
Not related.

◆ *Frank Stallone and Sylvester Stallone?*
Siblings.

◆ *Jean Stapleton and Maureen Stapleton?*
Not related.

Baby Names

What names were among the top 10 most popular baby girl names in the United States in both 1970 and 2000?

None, in fact. Here's the 1970 list:

1. Jennifer

2. Lisa

3. Kimberly

4. Michelle

5. Amy

6. Angela

7. Melissa

8. Tammy

9. Mary

10. Tracy

And the 2000 list:

1. Emily

2. Hannah

3. Madison

4. Ashley

5. Sarah

6. Alexis

7. Samantha

8. Jessica

9. Taylor

10. Elizabeth

What about boys' names?

There's a bit of overlap for the males, with Michael and Christopher appearing on both lists. Here's the list from 1970:

1. Michael

2. James

3. David

4. John

5. Robert

6. Christopher

7. William

8. Brian

9. Mark

10. Richard

And in 2000:

1. Jacob

2. Michael

3. Matthew

4. Joshua

5. Christopher

6. Nicholas

7. Andrew

8. Joseph

9. Tyler

10. Daniel

Won't giving my baby a unique and creative name help to distinguish him or her in the future?

Having common, ordinary first names didn't seem to hinder, say, Benjamin Franklin, Ronald Reagan, Thomas Edison, George Washington, or Nelson Mandela. Experts say that a child's name doesn't necessarily determine his or her destiny.

How unique will my baby girl be if I name her Unique?

Not completely. From 2000 to 2006, more than 1,000 newborn babies in the United States were named Unique. And that doesn't take into account the alternate spellings, such as Uneek.

Do celebrities influence the popularity of certain baby names?

Not as much as you'd think. ("Madonna" has never appeared in the top 10 names.) Researchers have found that parents remember who was the prettiest or most popular kids at their school and use those names for their own children.

Where did the name Nevaeh come from?

It is "heaven" spelled backward, and was number 150 in popularity in 2003. It is believed that the popularity of the name spread via the Internet after singer Sonny Sandoval mentioned that it was his daughter's name on an episode of MTV's *Cribs*.

Did parents actually name their child Ima Hogg?

Yes, Governor James Hogg of Texas christened his daughter Ima after a character in a poem written by his brother, Thomas Hogg. Contrary to popular legend, however, she did not have a sister named Ura.

What now-popular girls' name was inspired by a 1984 film?

Madison. In *Splash*, Daryl Hannah's character chose the name after seeing it on a street sign. Fifteen years later, Madison began showing up in the top five most popular baby names for girls (although it literally means "son of Maud").

Did some sports fanatic actually name his child ESPN after the cable network?

Not one, but at least three children have that name, according to government records.

Nicknames

On TV's Cheers, *what was Ernie Pantusso's response when asked how he became known as* Coach?

Because he "never flew first class."

How did playwright Neil Simon earn the nickname Doc?

As a child, one of his favorite toys was a stethoscope that came as part of a toy doctor play kit. He was rarely seen without it, so family members began to call him Doc.

What late rock bassist was known as The Ox?

John Entwistle of The Who.

How did Iggy Pop earn his unusual nickname?

From his high school band—the Iguanas. He was born James Jewel Osterburg.

What nickname does Fred Flintstone use while bowling?

Twinkle Toes.

Gangster Lester Nelson preferred to be called Big George, but was instead saddled with what other nickname?

Baby Face.

David Akeman was a country legend known to fans of the Grand Ole Opry and Hee-Haw by what nickname?

Stringbean.

What siblings were known to each other (and to family members and close friends) as Popo and Eppie?

Abigail Van Buren and Ann Landers, respectively.

Long before Elvis, what film star was known in Hollywood as "The King"?

Clark Gable, best known for portraying Rhett Butler in *Gone with the Wind.*

Who gave Marillion lead singer Fish his nickname?

A former landlord of his, who objected to the long periods of time he spent in the bath.

Who was referred to by the nickname Squidgy in a series of famously taped telephone conversations?

Princess Diana. Squidgy was the nickname given to her by James Gilbey, with whom she was having an affair.

The British Royal Family

What is Queen Elizabeth's full name?

Elizabeth Alexandra Mary Windsor. Her full title is a bit more unwieldy: Queen Elizabeth II, by the Grace of God, of the United Kingdom of Great Britain and Northern Ireland and of Her other Realms and Territories Queen, Head of the Commonwealth, Defender of the Faith. (Whew!)

Why is her husband called Prince Philip and not King Philip?

In the British monarchy, much like in poker, a King outranks a Queen. Because Elizabeth is Queen by virtue of her birthright, her husband is styled the Prince Consort in order to emphasize that she takes precedence.

How many children does the Queen have?

Four: Charles, the Prince of Wales; Anne, the Princess Royal; Andrew, the Duke of York; and Edward, the Earl of Wessex.

What does the Queen keep in that big purse?

Lipstick, a gold compact, a comb, and a handkerchief. On Sundays, she also carries a folded £5 note that she places in the collection plate during church service.

Was Lady Diana Spencer required to undergo an official physical examination before her engagement to Prince Charles?

Yes, but it wasn't to prove or disprove her virginity as was widely speculated; it was simply to ensure she was able to bear children, as one of her responsibilities as Princess would be to provide an heir.

Why isn't Charles's second wife known as the Princess of Wales?

The former Camilla Parker Bowles felt that the title was too closely associated with the late Princess Diana, so she chose to style herself the Duchess of Cornwall.

Was Diana planning to marry Dodi al-Fayed?

Apparently not. She'd only been seeing him for six weeks at the time of their fatal crash, and just days before the accident she'd told a close friend that she needed another husband like she needed "a bad rash."

Presidents and First Ladies

Who were the only two Federalist presidents?

George Washington and John Adams.

How many presidents have been married more than once?

Six: John Tyler, Millard Fillmore, Benjamin Harrison, Teddy Roosevelt, Woodrow Wilson, and Ronald Reagan. Of these, Reagan was the only one to be divorced; the others were widowers.

How old was Jackie Kennedy when she became First Lady?

Thirty-one. In fact, she was born later than the next six First Ladies to succeed her—Lady Bird Johnson, Pat Nixon, Betty Ford, Rosalynn Carter, Nancy Reagan, and Barbara Bush.

Who were the only four Whig presidents?

William Henry Harrison, John Tyler, Zachary Taylor, and Millard Fillmore.

What the heck is a Whig, anyway?

When the National Republican Party fell apart in the 1830s, the Whig Party was formed to oppose the Democrats. The Whigs enjoyed brief success, but disagreement on slavery and other issues caused the party's premature demise. By 1855, the Whig Party had dissolved, and most of its members joined the then-new Republican Party.

How many presidents had a matching set of initials (using the same letters for their first and last names)?

Actually, the number is smaller than you might think. It's two: Herbert Hoover and Ronald Reagan. What about Woodrow Wilson and Calvin Coolidge, you might ask? They both went by their middle names. Wilson's first name was Thomas, and Coolidge's was John.

What First Lady's "First 100 Days" cover for People magazine sold fewer than a million copies?

Hillary Clinton. This May 10, 1993, edition of *People* was the worst-selling issue of the decade.

Which presidents changed their names?

◆ Ulysses Simpson Grant was born Hiram Ulysses Grant.

◆ Dwight David Eisenhower was born David Dwight Eisenhower.

◆ Gerald Rudolph Ford Jr. was born Leslie Lynch King Jr.

◆ Bill Clinton was born William Jefferson Blythe, III.

Which U.S. presidents never had children of their own?

George Washington, James Madison, Andrew Jackson, James Knox Polk, and James Buchanan.

What First Lady shocked the nation when she revealed on TV's 60 Minutes that her children may have tried drugs and cheated on their spouses?

Betty Ford.

Eponyms

Are Peach Melba and Melba Toast named after the same person?

Yes. Both are named for the Australian superstar opera singer Nellie Melba.

Which states were named after British royalty?

Virginia was named in honor of Queen Elizabeth I, the "virgin queen." (West Virginia was named for Virginia, so we don't include it on the list.) Georgia was named for King George II, North and South Carolina for Charles I, and Maryland for Charles's wife, Queen Henrietta Maria.

Were any states named after members of the monarchy from other nations?

Yes. Louisiana was named after France's Louis XIV.

True or false?

Shrapnel was named after a British army officer named Henry Shrapnel, who invented an artillery shell?

True.

George Eastman named Kodak film after an American Indian who helped him during a trip to Texas?

False. He made up the name because he liked the "strong, incisive" sound of the letter K.

The saxophone was named after Antoine J. Sax?

True.

The guppy fish was named after an English scientist named Robert Guppy?

True.

The Rockola jukebox was named after its inventor, David Rockola?

True.

Who is the Phillips behind the Phillips screwdriver?

Henry F. Phillips, who patented both the crosshead screw and the tool used to drive it in 1936.

Was Julius Caesar "taken" from his mother, providing the name for the procedure that became known as the Caesarean section?

No. Stories circulated after his death suggesting that he was born in this fashion. This tale was false, but most etymologists believe that it inspired the name.

Well, then, was Caesar salad named for him?

No, again. The man behind this tasty dish was Mexican chef Caesar Cardini.

What about the Bloody Caesar cocktail?

No, that's zero for three. This beverage was devised in 1969 by Canadian bartender Walter Chell. The original recipe called for ground clams, as Clamato juice wasn't yet available.

The Wealthy

How did these philanthropists make their millions (or billions)?

◆ *John Jacob Astor?*
In the fur trade (and later with real estate).

◆ *James "Diamond Jim" Brady?*
In railroad equipment. (His nickname was the result of his love of jewelry.)

◆ *Andrew Carnegie?*
In the steel industry, as founder of U.S. Steel.

◆ *William Colgate?*
In the soap-making business.

◆ *Ezra Cornell?*
By developing telegraph systems.

◆ *Anthony Joseph Drexel?*
In banking.

◆ *J. P. Getty?*
In petroleum.

◆ *William Randolph Hearst?*
In journalism, as the owner of several newspapers.

◆ *Thomas Lipton?*
In the tea business.

◆ *Andrew W. Mellon?*
In banking and steel.

◆ *J. P. Morgan?*
Mostly railroads and steel, with interests in various other enterprises.

◆ *Alfred B. Nobel?*
In chemistry, as the inventor of dynamite.

◆ *Aristotle Onassis?*
In shipping.

◆ *H. Ross Perot?*
In data-processing services.

◆ *John D. Rockefeller?*
In petroleum, as founder of the Standard Oil Company.

◆ *Nathan Straus?*
In the retail industry, as co-owner of Macy's.

◆ *Cornelius Vanderbilt?*
In railroads and shipping.

SCIENCE 5

Animal Extremes

Do millipedes really have 1,000 legs?

No. The species with the most—*Illacme plenipes*—has up to 750. (This variety of millipede was thought to be extinct after 1926, but was rediscovered in 2005.)

What breed of dog is the fastest?

The greyhound. These canine speedsters can reach 45 mph over short distances.

How many vertebrae do giraffes have in their lengthy necks?

Seven. Most mammals, including humans, have seven. The largest giraffe vertebrae, however, can measure more than 12 inches long.

What's the largest animal on Earth?

The blue whale, which can exceed 150 tons.

What the largest animal to ever live on Earth?

Again, the blue whale. The largest known dinosaur was only about half as big.

What are the fastest birds?

In a dive, the peregrine falcon is the fastest (up to 200 mph), but a spine-tailed swift is said to be speedier in level flight.

What type of insect has the most venomous sting?

It's not a bee or a wasp, but an ant; specifically, the harvester ant. Twelve stings can be enough to kill a 5-pound mammal, and a single sting can cause intense pain in humans for several hours.

What's the loudest land animal?

With respect to your annoying neighbors, it's the howler monkey, whose cries can be heard up to 3 miles away.

The Solar System

What's the easiest way to determine if an object you're seeing in the sky is a star or a planet?

Look for the twinkle. Because stars emit light, they twinkle in the nighttime sky. Planets only reflect light, so while they're visible, they don't glimmer like stars.

What moon is larger in relation to its planet than any other in the solar system?

Earth's moon.

What's the difference between a meteor, a meteoroid, and a meteorite?

They all refer to small stones or metal bodies coming from space. While in space, they're called meteoroids. When they reach Earth's atmosphere and become "shooting stars," they're called meteors. And the few that make it intact to Earth's surface are called meteorites.

How many planets were discovered by Americans?

None. The answer used to be one—Pluto, spotted in 1930 by Clyde Tombaugh. But Pluto was demoted to "dwarf planet" status in 2006.

Why is it that people can spot Jupiter and Saturn in the sky, but Mercury (which is much closer to Earth) is tough to see?

Because of Mercury's proximity to the sun, it is difficult to define visually. The planet can only be spotted just before sunrise or just after sunset.

How many planetary moons are larger than Earth's moon?

Four. The largest is Ganymede (a moon of Jupiter), followed by Titan (Saturn), and then Callisto and Io (both orbiting Jupiter). In fact, both Ganymede and Titan are larger than the smallest planet, Mercury.

What's the whole deal with the waxing/waning and crescent/gibbous moon?

The waxing moon is going from new moon to full moon, while the waning moon is going from full moon back to new moon. A crescent moon is crescent-shaped, so it happens between a new moon and each quarter moon. A gibbous moon occurs between a quarter moon and a full moon.

Why don't Mercury and Venus have moons like all the other planets?

Because of their proximity to the sun. Any natural satellite orbiting too close to the surface would be pulled in by the planet's gravity, while any too far out would be dragged away by the sun's gravity.

What planet was originally known as *Georgium Sidus* and then *Herschel*?

Uranus. Astronomer William Herschel named the planet for King George III of England when he discovered it in 1781. Of course, Americans weren't keen to refer to the planet after the British monarch, so they called the planet Herschel after the man who discovered it.

Media Technology

Are the white "blips" onscreen in older movies a result of the lack of sound in those scenes?

Not exactly, but they're related. The corner "blips" were put there intentionally as an indication to the projector operator to change reels. This was often done in a silent part of the film to make the transition smoother.

What's the lifecycle of the average theatrical motion picture?

Typically, once a movie has exhausted itself at full-price cinemas, it goes to discount filmhouses. The next stop is home video, then pay-per-view cable, then premium cable stations, and then regular cable or network television.

Why aren't there any Channel 1 TV stations?

The earliest TVs did have a Channel 1, but after 1946, the FCC reassigned that signal bandwidth (44 to 50 MHz) for use with two-way radios.

Which U.S. TV station was the first to constantly show its logo in the corner of the screen?

Those annoying symbols are called "bugs" in the industry. CNN was the first American station to employ the tactic, which the news channel added to its coverage of the 1986 Challenger disaster to prevent other networks from "borrowing" exclusive footage.

Does the same guy do the voiceover on all movie trailers?

Not all, but many. Don LaFontaine's impossibly resonant voice has been heard in theaters across the country for the past 30 years intoning "In a world where ..." and "Now, more than ever ...."

Why aren't some very popular classic movies (like Gone with the Wind) available in widescreen?

Because they weren't filmed in widescreen. The format didn't become popular until the 1950s, when Hollywood became worried that TV would infringe on its turf and decided to increase the screen size to keep people coming to the movie theater.

Whatever happened to AM stereo?

It's still around, but it just isn't advertised very much in today's world, because the focus of AM radio is on content and signal power, not sound quality.

Why do most radio station ID jingles sound so similar?

Because the voices are those of the Johnny Mann Singers, who have been singing station IDs since the 1960s. The cast of voices changes occasionally, but the "melodies" remain the same.

Why do some AM radio stations sign off at sundown?

Radio waves travel farther at night due to the dissipation of the ionosphere after the sun goes down. As a result, the AM radio waves would be a jumble of noise if lower-power stations weren't required to end their broadcasting day early.

What's that loud "beep" tone that's played before national radio news broadcasts?

It's actually an audio signal that automatically switches a local radio station over to a national feed. While this can now be done digitally, listeners are so accustomed to the "bee-doop" sound that many networks continue to use it.

Birds

What's a bird doing when he cocks his head to the ground?

It's long been the rumor that they're listening for worms or insects, but they're actually looking for them. Birds' eyes are situated on each side of the head, and so the feathered creature must focus using one eye or the other to detect the movement.

Bald eagles have feathers on their heads, so why are they called bald?

It's short for piebald, meaning "white patch." The feathers on their heads are white.

Can ostriches fly?

No. But they can jog at 30 mph for several miles, and can exceed 40 mph over short distances if they're really in a hurry.

Why do some birds have beaks and others bills?

Land birds that eat plants and insects typically have pointed beaks that make it easier for them to feed. Waterfowl have bills that allow water to strain out while they're eating.

Do you have to travel to the South Pole to see penguins?

While Antarctica is home to many penguins, others can be found in certain spots throughout the Southern Hemisphere—in Africa, Australia, and South America. You won't find any at the North Pole, however. That's Santa's domain.

What's the scientific classification of a pterodactyl? Was it a bird?

Taxonomists group it with reptiles, although recent research has revealed that dinosaurs and birds may be more closely related than previously believed.

How do baby birds break out of their tough eggshells?

Young birds develop a "pipping muscle" in their necks that enables them to use their "egg tooth" on their beaks to work their way out of the shell (which weakens during incubation).

Why aren't seagulls attracted to bird feeders?

Their webbed feet make it difficult for them to perch, so gulls prefer to feed on flat surface areas (like parking lots and landfills).

What's the most populous type of bird in the world?

The domestic chicken. Estimates vary wildly, but the number is thought to be in the tens of billions worldwide.

Do some birds really explode after eating uncooked rice thrown at weddings?

No. It's an urban legend.

Math

What's the difference between a mean and an average?

Nothing. They're one and the same—the computational middle point of a series of numbers. It's a *median* that's different, as the middle number (or average of the two center numbers) in a series.

What's the origin of the math term algebra?

From the Arabic *al-jabr*, which means "restoring."

The fraction 22/7 is a close approximation of what mathematical constant?

Pi.

How long has the "pi" symbol (π) been used to represent pi?

Even though the ancient Greek symbol is nearly 3,000 years old, it was first used in this context only 300 years ago (in 1706).

What does it mean when a number is followed by an exclamation point, such as "4!"?

The symbol is called a factorial, and represents multiplying the number by every integer between itself and zero. In this case, $4! = 4 \times 3 \times 2 \times 1 = 24$.

Is 1 million the same number in the United States as it is in the United Kingdom?

Yes, but from there, it can get tricky. In America, 1,000 million is a billion, while in Britain it's a milliard. A U.S. trillion is a UK billion. (And yes, this discrepancy has caused problems in the sharing of information, which is why the U.S. system has become more and more prevalent internationally.)

What's the largest number that can be written using an eight-digit binary number?

255 (which would be 11111111).

What's the difference between braces, brackets, and parentheses?

(Parentheses are around this sentence.) [Brackets are around this sentence.] {Braces are around this sentence.}

What's the difference between a rectangle and a rhombus?

A rectangle has four right angles, while a rhombus has four equal sides. A square is both a rectangle and a rhombus.

What are the longest standard English words that can be spelled using only Roman numerals?

CIVIC, CIVIL, LIVID, MIMIC, and VIVID. (None of these contain letters in the proper sequence to be standalone Roman numerals, however.)

Doctors and Medicine

What is the difference between a physician and a doctor?

Every physician is a doctor, but not every doctor is a physician. Any person earning a Ph.D. in a nonmedical field (say, education) may be referred to as "doctor."

What's the difference between an "-ectomy," an "-ostomy," and an "-otomy"?

◆ An "-ectomy" means something is cut out or removed (as in a tonsillectomy).

◆ An "-ostomy" means a hole or opening is furnished (as in a colostomy).

◆ An "-otomy" means something is cut or sliced up (as in a lobotomy).

What is the difference between an MD and a DO?

Medical Doctors and Doctors of Osteopathy both undergo the same course of study and residency programs, and are subject to the same licensing standards. But DOs also have to complete a two-year program in Osteopathic Manipulative Medicine (hands-on treatment of the musculoskeletal system).

How was the stethoscope invented?

In 1816, a shy French physician was too timid to place his ear upon a woman's chest to listen to her heartbeat and breathing, so he constructed a tube using sheets of paper.

When did hospitals start letting fathers in the delivery room to witness the miracle of birth?

In 1965, Jay Hathaway of California traveled to Colorado to find a hospital that would allow him in the room when his wife gave birth. Shortly afterward, he co-founded the American Academy of Husband-Coached Childbirth.

What's the difference between an osteopath and a chiropractor?

Osteopathy is a complete system of medical care; for example, a DO can perform surgery. Chiropractic is an alternative form of treatment that relies primarily on spinal manipulation.

Why do I have to wait so long to see my doctor, even when I have an appointment?

Most doctors book their patients in 15-minute intervals, considered the ideal amount of time for a one-symptom patient. Invariably, some patients will take longer, and then (just like the airlines), some won't show up at all, so most doctors are forced to "overbook."

What's the difference between an intern, resident, chief resident, and attending physician?

◆ An intern is a recently graduated medical school student on his first year of the job.

◆ A resident is a second- or third-year worker.

◆ A chief resident is a post-grad in her fourth and final year of on-the-job training.

◆ An attending physician is a bona-fide licensed doctor on staff to whom the interns and residents report.

What medical specialists are typically the lowest paid among their physician peers?

Pediatricians. Conversely, orthopedic surgeons are often the highest paid.

The Stars

Why don't I see the Big Dipper on the list of constellations?

Because it's not a constellation. The Big Dipper is what's actually called an "asterism," or a cluster of stars. It's part of the constellation Ursa Major (the Big Bear).

How many stars are visible in the nighttime sky?

On a very clear night, and with very good eyesight (and nothing better to do), you might count 3,000 of them (or even more) in your line of sight. Don't lose your place!

What star is closer to Earth than any other?

The sun.

Yeah, but beyond that?

Proxima Centauri. It's 4.2 light years from Earth, so driving there at 70 mph would take you about 40 million years (if you drove 24 hours a day, and if there were a road). Of course, unless you're on Earth, references to "hours" and "miles" don't mean so much.

Does that mean Proxima Centauri is also the brightest star?

Not by a long shot. In fact, you can't even see it from Earth without a telescope. It's close, but it's dim.

So what's the brightest known star?

The Pistol Star, which is 10 million times brighter than the sun.

You can see that one from Earth, right?

No. When it comes to "apparent magnitude," the brightness of a star viewed from Earth, lower numbers are better. The Pistol Star has an apparent magnitude of 11, and the faintest stars that can be seen measure about a 6. The Hubble Space Telescope found the Pistol Star near the middle of our galaxy (the Milky Way) in 1997. It can't be seen from Earth.

What's the brightest star that we can see from Earth at night?

Sirius A. Even though it's twice as far from us as Proxima Centauri, it's easy to spot in the nighttime sky.

What are some of the weirder names for constellations?

Well, there's Tucana (the Toucan), Mensa (the Table), Caelum (the Chisel), Musca (the Fly), and Antila (the Air Pump).

I've never heard of those. Have I ever seen them?

Not unless you've been south of the Equator. They're all only visible from the Southern Hemisphere.

Chemistry and the Elements

What makes "atom" a poor name for the basis of chemistry?

It was named from the Greek for "indivisible," because atoms were once thought to be the most basic form of matter.

What was the first radioactive element ever found?

It depends on whom you ask. Uranium was discovered back in 1789, but wasn't known to be radioactive until 1896. Two years later, Marie and Pierre Curie identified radium, the first element that was discovered due to its radioactivity.

What are the cut-off points farther up on the Periodic Table?

Elements 1 through 83 are nonradioactive, while those from 84 and up are radioactive. Elements 1 through 94 are found in nature; those with higher atomic numbers have been created in laboratories.

Organic chemistry focuses on various compounds made from what key element?

Carbon.

Ten elements have atomic symbols that don't begin with the same letter as the element itself. Can you identify these?

- Na?
  Sodium.

- K?
  Potassium.

- Fe?
  Iron.

- Ag?
  Silver.

- Sn?
  Tin.

- Sb?
  Antimony.

- W?
  Tungsten.

- Au?
  Gold.

- Hg?
  Mercury.

- Pb?
  Lead.

What element was found to exist on the sun before it was found on Earth?

Helium. It was discovered as part of the sun's light spectrum in 1868, but not located on Earth until more than a quarter century later. (In fact, the element earned its name from *Helios*, the Greek god representing the sun.)

How many known elements are there?

At present, 115. The highest-numbered element is 118, and three (114, 116, and 118) have yet to be identified. Studies suggest that there may be around 125 total.

What was the central goal of the alchemy movement, which began over 2,000 years ago?

To find a way to convert other metals into gold. The medium believed to accomplish this was called the Philosopher's Stone.

Weather

Is it true that a storm is coming when a "ring" forms around the moon?

Often, yes. Reflected moonlight shining through icy, high-altitude clouds causes the visual ring. These same clouds are typically seen a few hours prior to a storm front.

What aspect of a thunderstorm is the most deadly?

The rain. Hail very rarely causes deaths, lightning may be fatal, and tornadoes certainly can be destructive. But flash floods caused by thunderstorms cause the most fatalities, at an average of about 150 each year in the United States.

What's the difference between a hurricane and a typhoon?

Basically, its location on the globe. If it's in the Atlantic Ocean or Gulf of Mexico, it's a hurricane. If it's in the Pacific Ocean or Indian Ocean, it's a typhoon.

What's a comfortable temperature in Celsius?

The easiest way to judge it is by remembering the 0/20/40 rule: 0°C is freezing (32°F), 20°C is room temperature (68°F), and 40°C is hot, what we call "triple-digits" (about 104°F).

If a tornado is approaching, is it smart to open your windows to help "equalize the pressure" in a building?

Absolutely not, say experts. Doing so does not lessen the likelihood of being hit or the damage caused. In fact, it creates additional hazards, because fierce winds whipping through opened windows may cause objects to fly around and cause much more destruction.

How does the National Weather Service define a "severe" thunderstorm?

It's defined as a storm with winds over 58 miles per hour, cloud-to-ground lightning, and hailstones larger than three quarters of an inch in diameter.

What is "heat lightning"?

It's actually the same as any other lightning. If a strike occurs 10 miles away or farther, we see the flash but don't hear the accompanying thunder. This is described as "heat lightning."

What's the difference between "partly sunny" and "partly cloudy"?

Either phrase refers to between 30 percent and 70 percent cloud coverage in the sky. If the past few days have been particularly gray and dreary, weathercasters will use the words "partly sunny" in order to add a subconscious note of cheer to their report.

When did hurricanes finally get male names?

In 1979, the World Meteorological Organization decided to begin alternating between male and female names for tropical storms. Hurricane Bob, which struck Louisiana in July 1979, was the first manly named 'cane to make landfall in the United States.

What do the different intensities of tornadoes on the Fujita scale mean?

An F0 funnel (the lowest) can damage billboards and knock over brick chimneys on rooftops. An F5 (the highest) tornado can strip the bark off trees and easily lift an automobile off the ground and toss it 100 meters. But unlike what you may have seen in the film *Twister*, the classification can't be made until after the tornado has run its course.

What is Doppler radar?

It's a system that gauges the frequencies of waves to determine the speed and direction of a traveling object. Weather forecasters regularly use them to track storms.

Computers

Charles Babbage's 1822 prototype Difference Engine, considered the first computer, was powered by what?

Steam. He never completed a full-scale version of the device, however.

Herman Hollerith's Tabulator machine—an early computer-type device—was first used (and proven successful) by what organization?

The U.S. Census Bureau. The machine calculated the results of the 1890 Census in record time. Hollerith later founded the Tabulating Machine Company, which merged into what's now International Business Machines—IBM.

What was the difference between MS-DOS and PC-DOS?

Both were versions of the same Disk Operating System once marketed by Microsoft. However, PC-DOS was contracted specifically for IBM computers, while MS-DOS was allotted to manufacturers of IBM clones.

What company sold more PCs than any other in the 1990s?

Packard Bell. The company merged with NEC and withdrew from the U.S. personal computer market in 1999, concentrating its efforts overseas.

What are the names of the five main consumer Windows operating system packages released by Microsoft from 1995 to 2006?

Windows 95, Windows 98, Windows Me, Windows XP, and Windows Vista. (Windows NT, Windows 2000, and Windows Server were not intended for personal use.)

What company produced an early personal computer known as the ...

♦ *ACE 1000?*
Franklin.

♦ *ADAM?*
Coleco.

♦ *Altair?*
MITS (Micro Instrumentation Telemetry Systems).

♦ *Geneva?*
Epson.

♦ *Lisa?*
Apple.

♦ *Rainbow?*
Digital Equipment Corporation (DEC).

♦ *TI-99/4?*
Texas Instruments.

♦ *TRS-80?*
Radio Shack (Tandy).

♦ *VIC-20?*
Commodore.

♦ *ZX80?*
Sinclair.

FOOD and DRINK 6

Sweets

Weren't Hydrox cookies just a knock-off of Oreos?

Actually, it was the other way around. Sunshine introduced their Hydrox-brand sandwich cookies (chocolate with a creme filling) in 1908; Nabisco followed with Oreos four years later. The Hydrox brand was discontinued in the 1990s.

How did Milk Duds get their name?

The "milk" part derives from the milk chocolate covering the caramel candies. The manufacturer found it impossible to get the candies to turn out in perfect spheres as was desired, so the shapes were referred to as "duds."

Which variety of Girl Scout Cookies sells the most?

Thin Mints are number one, followed closely by Samoas (or Caramel DeLites), with Peanut Butter Patties (or Tagalongs) in third place.

Where in Germany did German chocolate originate?

Actually, it was developed by an American English German. Huh? Samuel German, an England-born confectioner, came up with his chocolate recipe in Massachusetts in 1852.

What's the difference between chocolate cake and devil's food cake?

The key ingredient in devil's food cake is baking soda, which reacts to the acid in the cocoa and gives the cake its reddish hue.

Why is Boston cream pie called a pie when it's really a cake?

When this dessert was first created, cake pans weren't in use (they weren't compatible with wood-burning stoves), so pie tins were used instead. The layers of sponge cake necessary for Boston cream pie were prepared in pie tins, hence the name.

How did Toll House Cookies get their name?

Years ago in New England, toll houses were rest stops where travelers could enjoy a home-cooked meal and rest their horses. The owner of one such establishment added Nestlé semi-sweet chocolate pieces to a recipe for Butter Drop Do cookies, and a new treat was born.

What were the original Jell-O flavors?

When the gelatin dish was introduced in 1897, it was available in orange, strawberry, raspberry, and lemon.

What ice cream flavor is the most popular in the United States?

A 2006 Baskin-Robbins survey determined that Americans are pretty mundane when it comes to ice cream—vanilla is by far the biggest seller. Outside the United States, pralines and cream reigns supreme.

How "American" is apple pie?

Not very. Historical records show that apple pie was baked and regularly consumed in fourteenth-century England, long before the United States was founded. Apple pie was a particular favorite of Queen Elizabeth I.

How is the letter "M" placed on M&M candies?

The candies are placed into small indentations on a conveyor belt that runs them through a "printing press," which gently stamps the "M" on each one.

Beer and Wine

What lager was advertised for years as "the beer that made Milwaukee famous"?

Schlitz.

What's the difference between beer and malt liquor?

Purists will discuss minute details such as the difference between "top fermented" and "bottom fermented," but to make a long story short, malt liquor is sweeter-tasting than regular beer and has a higher alcohol content.

What shampoo brand of the 1970s–1980s was promoted as containing a cup of real beer in every bottle?

Body on Tap.

What 1983 Bally Midway video game had parents up in arms over its depiction of a bar full of beer-guzzling patrons?

Tapper. Bartenders must serve up Budweiser beer in the game; a later release of the game featured root beer.

What brand of beer was the first to be sold in cans?

Pabst was the first major brewery to can its suds, back in 1935. Schlitz was the first large brewery to employ what was called a "zip top" in 1963, which eliminated the need for a can opener.

What brand of beer was the focus of the 1977 motion picture Smokey and the Bandit?

Coors, which (at the time) was unavailable in the East.

What exactly is Cold Duck?

It was once the most popular sparkling wine in the United States. In 1937, the owner of Detroit's Pontchartrain Wine Cellars found a way to use up opened bottles of champagne before they went flat. He mixed the bubbly with red wine and a dash of sugar.

What children's story was pulled from a school reading list in Culver City, California, for its inclusion of a bottle of wine?

Little Red Riding Hood. In one rendition of the tale, the youngster's basket included a bottle of wine.

What brand of wine was advertised by legendary film director Orson Welles?

Paul Masson. His commercials pledging "We will sell no wine before its time" were well received.

Did Dom Perignon invent champagne?

No, but he was one of the first to market sparkling wine, even though the bubbles were considered an undesirable aberration.

Why do champagne bottles have indents at the bottom?

No, it's not to reduce the amount of beverage in the bottle. The shape provides extra strength against the pressure of the carbonation, which helps to keep the glass from breaking.

Shelf Life

IMPORTANT NOTE: These are guidelines; use your best judgment when dealing with food that could potentially cause illness when spoiled.

What bakery items last the longest?

While most have a safe lifespan of only a few days, cookies may remain fresh for two months after opening.

Which lasts longer, an open bottle of ketchup or an open bottle of mustard?

Mustard may be good for a year if kept refrigerated; ketchup has a much shorter lifespan when opened, perhaps two months.

What about that old standby sandwich-making pair, peanut butter and jelly?

Peanut butter will last six to nine months unopened, or three months opened, while jelly will last a year unopened, and six months opened and refrigerated.

Spices last forever, don't they?

Most begin to lose their flavor after about a year, but they're technically "good" for up to four years.

Do soft drinks keep longer in bottles or cans?

Cans are good for nearly a year after the expiration date, whereas plastic bottles may go flat after only three months.

What about salad dressings?

Most bottled dressings (including mayonnaise) will last three months in the refrigerator once opened.

Does an aerosol can of whipped cream last forever?

No. If it's real cream, it should be disposed of after a month in the refrigerator. The nondairy variety is safe for three months.

I've got some instant cocoa I didn't make last winter; is it still good this winter?

Yes. Unopened packages will last indefinitely.

What vegetables last the longest when refrigerated?

Artichokes, cabbage, iceberg lettuce, onions, potatoes, rutabagas, and turnips might last for two weeks.

Restaurant Names

I thought Popeye loved spinach. How did his name get attached to Popeye's Fried Chicken?

Actually, the restaurant was named for Popeye Doyle, the character that won an Oscar for Gene Hackman from the film *The French Connection*. (Still, the company has licensed the use of images of Popeye the Sailor Man in its advertising.)

But Arby's was named after R. B. for "roast beef," right?

Yes and no. It was for R. B., but those initials stood for the founders, the Raffell Brothers.

How did Pizza Hut get its name?

When the Carney brothers started a pizzeria in Wichita in 1958, the sign above the building only accommodated nine letters. They wanted it to be called Pizza ... something, and because the structure was shaped like a hut ....

Were any other restaurant chains named after architectural limitations?

Yes. The story goes that Jack-in-the-Box was inspired due to an "ugly" air vent on the original restaurant's roof. The founders thought to cover up the blemish by topping it with a clown's face and turning it into a huge jack-in-the-box.

How did Red Lobster earn its colorful name?

Thanks to the man who printed their menus. Founder Bill Darden had previously run a restaurant called the Green Frog, so it was suggested that his new venture—a seafood eatery—be called Red Lobster.

Which regal name came first: Burger King or Dairy Queen?

The first Burger King restaurant opened in 1954, while the first Dairy Queen began operation way back in 1940.

Did Wendy's founder Dave Thomas really have a daughter named Wendy?

Her real name was (and still is) Melinda. As a youngster, her siblings had difficulty pronouncing her name, so they called her Wendy.

Did a church bell, school bell, or dinner bell inspire the name of Taco Bell?

None of the above. The truth is a bit more mundane. The fast-food chain was named for its founder, Glen Bell.

Richard Woodruff inspired the name of what restaurant chain?

Big Boy. As a husky six-year-old, he would do odd jobs around Bob Wian's restaurant in exchange for a double-decker burger. The Big Boy character is based on him.

Vitamins and Minerals

There are vitamins A, B, C, D, E, and K. What happened to the missing letters?

They belong to substances that were originally identified as vitamins, but were later reclassified. Vitamin G, for instance, is now known as riboflavin (vitamin B₂).

In 1995, what shape was removed from Flintstones Vitamins to make room for Betty Rubble?

The Flint-mobile.

Is there one particular food that's as good for you as taking a multi-vitamin?

No, but Popeye was on the right track: spinach is very close. It contains vitamins A, B₁, B₂, B₃, B₆, C, E, and K, as well as calcium, folic acid, iron, magnesium, potassium, and high fiber. (And it has no fat and no cholesterol.)

What vitamin can the human body generate on its own when the skin is exposed to the sun?

Vitamin D.

Who calculates those RDAs (Recommended Daily Allowances) for known vitamins and minerals?

The National Academy of Sciences. The organization is tasked with performing scientific research on request from the federal government.

Extra amounts of what vitamin are recommended for people who smoke?

Vitamin C. An increase of about 40 percent over the standard RDA is suggested to help smokers maintain proper plasma and oxygen levels in the blood.

The brand name of what vitamin is also its recommended dosage?

One-a-Day.

The recommended daily allowance of what common dietary supplement is higher for women than for men?

Iron. Women of child-bearing age require about twice as much iron as men.

Veggie Foods

What is tofu made of?

Bean curd. Soymilk made from soybeans is processed into curds and whey, and the curds are then formed into tofu.

What about tempeh?

Similar to tofu, tempeh is made from cooked, fermented soybeans.

Hummus?

Ground-up chickpeas, often flavored with garlic.

And poi?

It's made from the corm (stem) of the taro plant, which is mashed into a paste.

Couscous?

This dish is made from small grains of wheat that have been coated with flour.

Porridge?

Porridge is a hot dish made by boiling a grain—like oats, rice, or wheat—in milk and/or water.

Grits?

Grits is a porridge made from coarsely ground corn kernels.

Seitan (wheat gluten)?

It's made by removing the starch from wheat dough, leaving only the gluten. (And yes, the word "glue" comes from the same Latin root.)

Breakfast

In diner slang, the phrase "wreck a pair" tells the cook to do what?

Scramble two eggs.

What Michigan city is the home of two of America's biggest brand names in cereals, Post and Kellogg's?

Battle Creek. It's widely known by the nickname Cereal City.

There are three cereals in General Mills's "monster" cereal line, right?

Yes. Booberry, Count Chocula, and Frankenberry. But two others have come and gone: Fruit Brute and Yummy Mummy were short-lived inclusions.

What's the only Lucky Charms marshmallow that hasn't changed since the cereal's introduction?

Pink hearts is the only original "marbit" to remain exactly the same since 1964.

Is Jimmy Dean (the sausage company) and Jimmy Dean (country vocalist) the same person?

Yes. In fact, the profits from his hit songs (including the Grammy-winning 1962 single "Big Bad John") helped finance the founding of Dean's sausage company in 1969.

What's the difference between a Western Omelet and a Denver Omelet?

Just the terminology. Both are a mixture of eggs, ham, onion, cheese, and green pepper. Those in western states refer to it as a Denver Omelet, while east of the Mississippi, it's a Western Omelet.

It doesn't contain grapes or nuts, so why is that cereal called Grape-Nuts?

When Post introduced the cereal in 1898, it was made with maltose, which was confused with dextrose ("grape sugar"). The "nuts" part of the name is due to the product's slightly nutty flavor.

Was Tang developed specially for NASA?

No. It was introduced by General Mills back in 1957, before the first humans visited space. The drink mix gained fame a few years later, when NASA selected it for use aboard manned space flights.

Was the dish eggs benedict named after Benedict Arnold?

No. There is some controversy behind the origin of the dish, but most reliable sources credit a hung-over Wall Street broker named Lemuel Benedict, who staggered into the Waldorf Astoria one morning in 1894 and ordered "some buttered toast, crisp bacon, two poached eggs, and a hooker of hollandaise sauce."

What's the difference between American bacon and Canadian bacon?

American bacon comes from the belly of the pig and is smoked and cured. Canadian bacon is made from pork loin and is much leaner.

What was the name of the talking toaster who promoted Pop Tarts breakfast pastries?

Milton.

In the 1993 film **Falling Down,** *what fictional fast-food restaurant draws the ire of Michael Douglas when it refuses to serve him breakfast?*

Whammy Burger.

Liquor

What's the difference between whiskey (with an "e") and whisky (without one)?

Generally, the American-made beverage is known as whiskey, while the liquor from other nations is more often called whisky.

Did Jack Daniels die after drinking a bad batch of his own whiskey?

No, it was more complicated than that. He forgot the combination to his office safe, and injured his foot by kicking it in frustration. The wound eventually led to gangrene, and the disease proved fatal.

What's the difference between Scotch and Bourbon?

In order to be labeled Scotch, the whisky must have been distilled and matured in Scotland. Bourbon must be produced in the United States and contain a minimum of 51 percent corn grain.

What liquor became such a burden to British citizens in the 1700s that heavy taxes were levied to reduce its consumption?

Gin.

What's the relationship between the percentage of alcohol and "proof" numbers?

Exactly half. Liquor that is 80 proof is 40 percent alcohol.

So 200 proof alcohol is pure alcohol?

Yes, but it's impossible to sustain, because pure alcohol will pull moisture from the air and dilute itself to 97 percent.

What TV legend's grandfather was one of the founders of Bacardi rum?

Desi Arnaz of *I Love Lucy*.

For over half a century, a mysterious visitor has left three roses and a half-full bottle of what alcohol on Edgar Allan Poe's gravesite every year on his birthday?

Cognac. In 2007, it was revealed as a stunt intended to focus attention on preservation of the Baltimore cemetery where Poe's body is buried.

Why is a Bloody Mary served with a celery stalk?

This tradition dates back to the 1960s when a guest at Chicago's Ambassador East Hotel grew impatient while waiting for a swizzle stick and grabbed a piece of celery off a nearby garnish tray.

Why are liquor stores called "package stores" in some locales?

This is due to laws that require the bottles to be packaged up in paper bags before they leave the store.

Condiments

In what city is Pace picante sauce, famous for its "New York City?!" advertisements, produced?

San Antonio, Texas.

How was Worcestershire sauce invented?

The Governor of Bengal asked British chemists to reproduce his favorite Indian food sauce. They failed, and the rejected mixture sat in a cellar for two years. The flavor changed in the aging process, and the sauce was given a new name.

What odd colors of ketchup did Heinz begin marketing in the late 1990s?

Blastin' Green, Funky Purple, Passion Pink, Awesome Orange, and Totally Teal were the radical colors available in Heinz's EZ Squirt line.

What exactly is horseradish?

It's a member of the mustard family, along with cauliflower, kale, and Brussels sprouts. The large white tubular root is much bigger than a traditional radish, so it was named "horse" radish in order to properly describe the hugeness of the object.

Why are salt and pepper the traditional condiments found on restaurant tables?

One of the five areas of taste on the tongue is "salt," so it tastes pretty good on everything to most people. Pepper has been popular for 2,000 years; it added some zest to otherwise bland food, and also concealed the flavor of spoiled food in those prerefrigeration days. Salt and pepper are also two of the least-expensive spices.

I've seen "mace" in the spice aisle; what is it?

It's unrelated to the self-defense spray you buy in a can. Mace comes from the same seed as nutmeg, and is the spice responsible for giving doughnut shops their distinctive, doughnutty aroma.

Why are some ethnic cuisines so spicy?

Cultures in warmer climates (Italy, India, the Middle East, Mexico) use heavy doses of garlic, onion, oregano, cumin, and allspice because they have high antimicrobial properties and help prevent food spoilage.

What comedian tried to capitalize on his TV fame by bottling Backyard Barbecue Sauce?

Jeff Foxworthy.

What's the difference between "ketchup" and "catsup"?

Nothing but spelling. The condiment was called "ke-tsiap" in seventeenth-century China, and when it made its way to England, the Brits anglicized the name first to "catchup" and then to "ketchup." When competing companies started marketing the product in the United States, they alternated the spelling between "ketchup" and "catsup."

On what continent would you find the Thousand Islands for which the salad dressing is named?

North America. They're located in Lake Ontario.

What's the meaning of the tortoise-shell symbol on bottles of Kikkoman soy sauce?

The character translates to the number 10,000.

Is there a real Hidden Valley Ranch?

Sure—the 120-acre facility first opened in 1954 in Santa Barbara County, California. And yes, it's where the salad dressing was first made.

The McIlhenny Company is the only licensed producer of what sauce?

Tabasco Sauce.

Fairy Tales, Fables, and Nursery Rhymes

Did the Brothers Grimm write Grimm's Fairy Tales?

Yes and no. German siblings Jacob and Wilhelm Grimm worked as librarians and began collecting folktales in 1806 with the idea of publishing them in a book. So they compiled the book, but they didn't actually "write" the majority of the stories.

Fable-writer Aesop lived in what ancient land some 2,500 years ago?

Greece. His place of birth is uncertain, however. Most believe he was from Thrace, but others claim he was from Egypt or Ethiopia.

Who wrote The Little Mermaid *and* The Ugly Duckling?

Hans Christian Andersen.

Is "Ring Around the Rosie" really about the Black Plague?

No. This story, like many other similar "explanations" of old nursery rhymes, was a twentieth-century theory with no basis in fact.

Was there really a Mother Goose?

Several folks have laid claim to being the fairy-tale author (including a woman named Mary Goose who lived in Boston during the 1600s), but so far there is no confirmation as to who actually wrote those stories.

What happened to the heroes in the resolutions of the original Grimm Brothers' versions of these fairy tales?

◆ *The Three Little Pigs?*
The wolf, unable to blow down the brick house, tries to enter via the chimney but falls into a cauldron of boiling water.

◆ *Little Red Riding Hood?*
The hunter cuts open the wolf, and Red and her grandmother spring from his stomach unharmed.

◆ *Hansel and Gretel?*
After shoving her into the oven, the kids steal the witch's jewels, then meet up with their father in the woods.

In 1936, Sergei Prokofiev composed a clever musical version of what fairy tale?

Peter and the Wolf. Specific instruments were used to mimic each of the story's characters.

According to the nursery rhyme of the same name, **Who Killed Cock Robin?**

The sparrow (with his bow and arrow).

The Bible

In what language was the Bible originally written?

The Old Testament was primarily composed in Hebrew, while most of the New Testament was written in Greek.

What American icon bears an inscription from Leviticus, Chapter 25?

The Liberty Bell. It reads "Proclaim liberty throughout all the land unto all the inhabitants thereof."

Where do the Ten Commandments appear in the Bible?

In two spots, actually: Exodus 20:17 and Deuteronomy 5:6–21.

Are the Gideon Bibles seen in hotel rooms and other public places free for the taking?

No. Gideons International pays for each of them to be placed there for reading by visitors.

Was the Bible the first book printed on the Gutenberg printing press?

Yes. Beginning in 1450, Gutenberg printed 200 copies of the Bible in Latin.

What's the only breed of dog mentioned by name in the King James Version of the Bible?

The greyhound (Proverbs 30:29–31).

The Bible Belt is concentrated in which quadrant of the United States?

The Southeast. It stretches from Texas to Virginia.

Are these Bible quotes or not?

◆ *"Fools rush in where angels fear to tread."*
Not (from an essay by Alexander Pope).

◆ *"... money is the root of all evil."*
Bible (I Timothy).

◆ *"God helps those who help themselves."*
Not (attributed to Benjamin Franklin).

◆ *"Spare the rod and spoil the child."*
Not (from English poet Samuel Butler).

◆ *"With God, all things are possible."*
Bible (Matthew).

◆ *"Physician, heal thyself."*
Bible (Luke).

Newspapers

What comic strip, centered around a newspaper staffed by birds, hit home for those who worked on the papers in which the strip appeared?

Shoe.

In 1887, what became the first newspaper headed by William Randolph Hearst?

The San Francisco Examiner.

Which are more popular, morning newspapers or evening newspapers?

Up through 1980, evening newspapers had a higher circulation, but their numbers have dipped precipitously. Today, morning papers outsell their evening counterparts six to one.

What newspaper printed the famous incorrect headline "Dewey Defeats Truman"?

The Chicago Daily Tribune was the culprit. In the paper's defense, most regular staffers were out on strike, and the skeleton crew had to rely on the slow election returns coming in via teletype.

What is the difference between a tabloid and a broadsheet?

It's all in the presentation. A tabloid paper measures about 17"×11" and reads like a book. Broadsheets measure 29½"×23½" and are folded in half vertically.

As of 2007, what were the only two U.S. newspapers with a national circulation in excess of 2 million?

USA Today and *The Wall Street Journal.*

What part of a newspaper is the "rotogravure"?

Technically, the term refers to a printing process, but in general terms it refers to all the special ad inserts and news magazines inserted into your Sunday newspaper.

What California city's newspaper is known by the odd name The Bee?

Sacramento.

Shakespeare

Did William Shakespeare have any children?

Yes. He married Anne Hathaway when he was 18, and six months later their daughter Susanna was born. (Yes, Anne was already in the family way when the couple officially tied the knot.) Two years later, she gave birth to twins, son Hamnet and daughter Judith.

Shakespeare's work became so famous that people began to refer to him as "The Bard." What exactly is a bard?

Bard originally referred to a trained Celtic scholar who wrote and performed lyrical works. Later, the word simply came to mean "poet."

How did the Black Plague affect Shakespeare?

It caused the death of his only son, but it also gave him time to focus on writing some of his most famous plays as he hibernated indoors while the sickness ravaged London.

What are some of the commonly used words coined by Shakespeare?

The Bard had an amazing vocabulary of over 28,000 words (the average adult knows about 10,000), and the first time many of these words first appeared in print were in his writings. The list includes assassinate, gossip, luggage, and even puke.

Didn't he also invent some phrases that we still use today?

Sure. "Tower of strength," "budge an inch," "in my heart of hearts," "what is done is done," and "the long and short of it" all first appeared in Shakespeare's plays.

Was Shakespeare strictly a playwright?

No. He considered himself a poet. And he'd been an actor before he got into the play writing mode. Years later, he played parts in his own plays onstage in front of Queen Elizabeth I and King James I.

Was Shakespeare anti-Semitic?

No one can say for sure, but the Bard did create the evil, money-lending character Shylock in *The Merchant of Venice* whose name has since become used as a derisive term for a loan shark.

Did Shakespeare have a sense of humor?

Indeed. In fact, he's widely credited with inventing the "knock knock" joke. We don't want to spoil the punch line by revealing it here, so you'll have to check it out for yourself in Act Two, Scene Three of *Macbeth*.

Is "Shakespeare" the correct spelling of his name?

Apparently, William wasn't certain himself. The six existing authenticated examples of his signature vary greatly, from Shakspere to Shaksper to Shakspeare.

Magazine Covers

Who appeared on the first cover of ...

- ◆ *Rolling Stone?*
  John Lennon.

- ◆ *Playboy?*
  Marilyn Monroe.

◆ *Entertainment Weekly?*
k.d. lang

◆ *People?*
Mia Farrow.

◆ *Jane?*
Drew Barrymore.

◆ *Rosie?*
Fran Drescher.

◆ *TV Guide?*
Lucille Ball (and Desi Arnaz Jr).

◆ *Sports Illustrated?*
Eddie Mathews.

◆ *Spin?*
Madonna.

◆ Ms.?
Wonder Woman.

Science Fiction

Who is widely considered to be the first author to specialize in science-fiction books?

Jules Verne.

Was George Orwell alive to see if his book
Nineteen Eighty-Four *would prove prophetic?*

No. Tuberculosis took his life in 1950 at the age of 46.

What sci-fi TV show of the mid-1970s was set on
Moonbase Alpha?

Space: 1999.

The most popular sci-fi magazine of its day,
Astounding Science Fiction, *is now known by*
what different title?

Analog.

What **Friends** *actor took on the role of Major Don*
West in the 1998 film update of the TV sitcom
Lost in Space?

Matt LeBlanc.

Was sci-fi legend Isaac Asimov really afraid of
flying?

Yes.

At what age were adults put to death in the 1976 motion picture **Logan's Run?**

Thirty.

What just-about-to-break-out actress portrayed Holly in that film?

Farrah Fawcett-Majors. She'd previously appeared on a few episodes of her then-husband's sci-fi TV show, *The Six Million Dollar Man*.

Ray Bradbury's **Fahrenheit 451** *was titled after the temperature at which what common item will burst into flame?*

Paper. The story describes futuristic "firemen" who burn books.

Which member of the original **Star Trek** *cast once said he'd been given telepathic messages by a UFO in the Mojave Desert?*

William Shatner.

Poetry

The short-lived game show **Rhyme & Reason** *was created specially to showcase the poetic talent of what comedian?*

Nipsey Russell.

A view from what natural landmark inspired Katharine Lee Bates to write the poem "America the Beautiful" in 1893?

Pikes Peak.

What 1977 Terry Gilliam film was named after a Lewis Carroll poem?

Jabberwocky.

Referred to often in his novels, what once-fictional collection of Dean Koontz poems became real when he published it in a 2003 limited edition?

The Book of Counted Sorrows.

What 1970s–1980s game show opened with the announcer reciting a short poem written by a viewer?

Card Sharks.

?

What mild-mannered comedian held oversized flowers in his hands while reciting poetry on TV's Laugh-In?

Henry Gibson.

?

What 1982 Australian film was based on an epic poem by A. B. "Banjo" Patterson?

The Man from Snowy River.

?

What colorful character was poet F. Gelett Burgess referring to when he wrote, "I'd rather see than be one"?

A purple cow.

Comic Strips and Comic Books

Lois Flagston of Hi & Lois *is the sister of what other famous comic-strip character?*

Beetle Bailey.

From oldest to youngest, what are the names of the kids in The Family Circus?

Billy, Jeffy, Dolly, and P. J.—and their parents are Bill and Thelma.

What three "little" characters appeared in Harvey comic books?

Little Audrey, Little Dot, and Little Lotta.

The initials in DC Comics stand for what?

Detective Comics. (So, yes, the company's name is Detective Comics Comics.)

What's the middle name of late Peanuts *artist Charles M. Schulz?*

Monroe.

What are the last names of the characters in the Peanuts comic strip?

Over the course of the comic strip, we learn the last names of Charlie and Sally (Brown); Linus, Lucy, and Rerun (Van Pelt); Peppermint Patty (Reichardt); and Violet (Gray). In the animated special *You're in the Super Bowl, Charlie Brown*, we are given last names for Marcie (Johnson) and Franklin (Armstrong). But a few characters, including Pig-Pen, are never given "real" names.

The "R" on Archie Andrews's letterman jacket represents the name of his high school, which is located in what town?

Riverdale.

What Christmas character was first introduced in 1939 in a promotional giveaway comic book for Montgomery Ward stores?

Rudolph the Red-Nosed Reindeer.

Which came first, Buster Brown shoes or the Buster Brown comic-strip character?

The comic strip premiered in 1902, and Buster was officially licensed to the Brown Shoe Company (named for its founder, not for the character) two years later.

What comic-strip character lends his name to bags of prepackaged snack "fries" that a pub fixture like him would undoubtedly enjoy?

Andy Capp.

What 1990 film was shot using primarily only the eight colors used in the comic strip on which it was based?

Dick Tracy. The colors were black, white, yellow, orange, red, green, blue, and purple.

Speedy is the name of what comic-book character's young sidekick?

The Green Arrow.

American Folklore

Were the following characters real or fictional?

♦ *Johnny Appleseed?*
Real. His name was John Chapman.

♦ *Buffalo Bill?*
Real.

◆ *Pecos Bill?*
Fictional.

◆ *Daniel Boone?*
Real.

◆ *Paul Bunyan?*
Fictional.

◆ *Ichabod Crane?*
Fictional.

◆ *Davy Crockett?*
Real, though not the same guy you know from the old Disney
TV show.

◆ *John Henry?*
Fictional.

◆ *Calamity Jane?*
Real. Her name was Martha Canary.

◆ *Casey Jones?*
Real.

◆ *Joe Magarac?*
Fictional.

◆ *Annie Oakley?*
Real. And a darned good shot, too.

◆ *Rip Van Winkle?*
Fictional.

Language

Do young children really pick up foreign languages better than teenagers and adults?

Studies have shown that, yes, they do, and that the cut-off point is typically the beginning of the teenage years. Given equivalent training, a student who began learning a foreign language at the age of eight will usually sound more "natural" than one who waited until college to start.

What three foreign-language classes are the over- whelming choices for American high school students?

Spanish is number one, followed by French, with German a distant third. Fourth on the list is a "dead" language—Latin.

What is considered the most difficult English sound for foreign students to master?

"Th." Few other languages employ the sound, and the pronun- ciation subtleties in words like "three," "the," and "isthmus" can prove difficult to distinguish.

English is the most-used language in the United States, while Spanish is second. What's third?

American Sign Language.

What is the official language of aviation?

In 2001, the International Civil Aviation Organization (ICAO) determined that English would from then on be the standardized language of air travel. They issued a directive that stated all aviation personnel—pilots, flight crews, and air traffic controllers—must pass an English proficiency test.

What does RSVP mean?

Literally, it is French for "répondez, s'il vous plâit," which means "Reply, if you please." So technically, an invitation reading "RSVP, please" contains a redundancy.

While Sesame Street *focuses on Spanish as a second language, Fred Rogers of* Mr. Rogers' Neighborhood *sometimes spoke what foreign tongue?*

French. He used it occasionally on his long-running children's TV show.

What is the difference between "i.e." and "e.g."?

♦ i.e. is Latin for *id est*, which means "that is." You'd use i.e. if you want to present your statement in other words.

♦ e.g. is Latin for *exempli gratia*, and is used when you give an example to amplify your statement.

TRAVEL and PLACES 8

Automobiles

What NFL expansion team was forced to change its logo after an automotive company threatened a lawsuit?

The Jacksonville Jaguars, whose initial design too closely resembled that of Jaguar Motors.

What American automaker became the top-selling "foreign" brand in China in 2006?

General Motors.

In 1987, what luxury automaker was the first American company to offer compact disc players in its vehicles?

Lincoln. A CD player was offered as an option on 1988 Town Cars.

Did Adolf Hitler design the Volkswagen Beetle?

No, but he did commission the design of "the people's car."

What European automaker purchased a controlling interest in American Motors in 1979, saving it from bankruptcy?

Renault.

What brand of tires did Henry Ford choose for his very first mass-produced automobiles?

Firestone.

In 1982, what Japanese automaker became the first to open an assembly plant for their automobiles on U.S. soil?

Honda, in Marysville, Ohio. Today, three of every four Hondas sold in the United States are built domestically.

What Datsun "Z-car" was only made for one model year, 1974?

The 260Z. The successor to the 240Z experienced engine problems, resulting in a revised 280Z model for 1975.

What Dodge car was updated and put on sale in January 1999 to become the first automobile given a 2000 model year designation?

The Neon.

Were Ford Model Ts available in "any color, as long as it's black"?

Actually, they were made in a variety of colors early and late in the model's run. While most were black, there were factory-painted Model Ts in green, blue, and even red.

Flags

What's the only nation to have a single-color flag, and what color is it?

Libya, whose flag is solid green.

How many stars and stripes appeared on the 1813 U.S. flag first christened the "Star Spangled Banner"?

Fifteen stars and 15 stripes. Later, Congress reduced the number of stripes back to 13 and used extra stars to indicate additional states joining the Union.

The object of what Milton Bradley board game is to capture the opponent's flag?

Stratego.

What's the only state flag that has more than four sides?

Ohio's flag, which is a five-sided burgee shape.

What's the procedure for flying a flag at half-staff?

The flag has to be hoisted to the top first, then lowered to the halfway point. When taken down, the flag should also be hoisted to the top before being lowered for removal.

The area in the upper left-hand quadrant of a flag—such as the blue field with stars on the U.S. flag—is known by what proper name?

The canton.

Using this term, what state flag features the British Union Jack in its canton?

Hawaii.

In 1924, Alvin "Shipwreck" Kelly became the first to attempt what flag-related stunt?

Flagpole sitting. His first attempt lasted 13 hours and 13 minutes. (The current record stands at nearly 200 days.)

Does the American flag have six white stripes or six red stripes?

Six white stripes. There are seven red stripes, including the ones on the very top and very bottom of the flag.

What popular dish is said to represent the colors of Italy's flag?

Pizza margherita: red (tomato sauce), white (mozzarella cheese), and green (basil).

Boats and Ships

The Grand Turk *is perhaps the most famous in the series of ships used as the logo for what brand name?*

Old Spice.

What name did Fred Flintstone and Barney Rubble come up with for a houseboat they won on a game show?

Unable to decide between *Nautical Lady* and *Queen of the Sea*, they combined the two and called the boat *NauSea*.

How many total "hits" does it take to destroy an opponent's fleet in the game of Battleship?

Seventeen.

What do the initials R.M.S.—as in R.M.S. Titanic—stand for?

Royal Mail Ship.

What's the name of the ship captained by cereal hero Cap'n Crunch?

The S.S. *Guppy*.

The word kayak, meaning a type of lightweight canoe, is an example of what type of wordplay?

A palindrome—a word or phrase that reads the same forward and backward.

In what year did six versions of "The Banana Boat Song" hit the Top 25?

1957.

Is a ship's captain legally authorized to perform marriage ceremonies?

Only if he's an ordained minister or Justice of the Peace.

How does the U.S. Navy choose names for its ships?

There's no set rule, but in most cases …

◆ Aircraft carriers are named after public officials (such as presidents).

◆ Battleships are named after states.

◆ Cruisers get their names from famous battles.

◆ Destroyers are named for famous people.

◆ Minesweepers get their names from birds.

What exactly is a "poop deck"?

The poop deck is the roof of the poop cabin, which is located on the stern and extends from the mizzenmast aft. The word is derived from the Latin *puppis*, which means "stern."

Amusement Parks

What California attraction promotes itself as "America's Oldest Themed Amusement Park"?

Knott's Berry Farm.

What are the six flags that fly over the first Six Flags park, Six Flags Over Texas?

The flags represent the six independent nations that have controlled Texas over its history: France, Spain, Mexico, the Republic of Texas, the Confederate States of America, and the United States of America.

What Midwest amusement park has more roller coasters than any other facility in the world?

Cedar Point, located in Sandusky, Ohio, with 17.

Both The Partridge Family *and* The Brady Bunch *filmed episodes in what then-new Ohio amusement park?*

Kings Island. The park's parent company, Paramount, also produced both television shows.

What bald actor played a crazed robotic cowboy at an adult amusement park in the 1973 film Westworld?

Yul Brynner.

In what direction do the vast majority of American carousels turn, clockwise or counter-clockwise?

Counter-clockwise. Elsewhere in the world, they usually travel clockwise.

The organization known as A.C.E. is dedicated to fans of what amusement park ride?

Roller coasters (American Coaster Enthusiasts).

In what city was the first foreign Disney theme park opened?

Tokyo, Japan, in 1983. A second international Disney park opened in Paris in 1992, and a third in Hong Kong in 2005.

U.S. States

What's the only U.S. state ...

♦ *... that borders only one other state?*
Maine.

♦ *... that borders both the Atlantic Ocean and the Gulf of Mexico?*
Florida.

♦ *... that borders both the Atlantic Ocean and a Great Lake?*
New York.

♦ *... that borders three Canadian provinces?*
Montana.

♦ *... with a predominantly green flag?*
Washington.

♦ *... whose flag has a different design on each side?*
Oregon.

♦ *... divided into parishes instead of counties?*
Louisiana.

♦ *... whose name begins (but does not end) with the letter A?*
Arkansas.

♦ *... to join the Union by way of presidential proclamation?*
West Virginia.

♦ *... with a population smaller than Washington, D.C.?*
Wyoming.

♦ *... with a unicameral (one-house) state legislature?*
Nebraska.

◆ *... that does not require its voters to register?*
North Dakota.

◆ *... that is home to two Federal Reserve Banks?*
Missouri (in Kansas City and St. Louis).

Continents

You'll probably notice a pattern here! Which continent is ...

◆ *... the largest?*
Asia, with about 30 percent of the land area on Earth.

◆ *... the smallest?*
Australia, with only about 5 percent of Earth's land area.

◆ *... the most populated?*
Asia, with nearly 4 billion people.

◆ *... the least populated?*
Antarctica, with no native population. Of the populated continents, Australia is last with 20 million people (less than half of 1 percent of Earth's total).

◆ *... the most crowded?*
Asia, with more than 215 people per square mile.

◆ *... the least crowded?*
Antarctica, with zero. Of the populated continents, it's Australia, with 6.5 people per square mile.

◆ *... home to the highest point of land on Earth?*
Asia, with Mount Everest.

◆ *... home to the lowest point of land on Earth?*
Antarctica. Under all that ice, you'll find land that's 8,327 feet (more than a mile and a half) below sea level.

◆ *... driest?*
Antarctica. Yes, really. The ice that's there has gathered over many centuries, and Antarctica has less precipitation than any other continent.

◆ *... wettest?*
Okay, you got us. The wettest continent is South America.

Aircraft

In what U.S. state did the first regularly scheduled passenger airline service begin in 1914?

Florida (between St. Petersburg and Tampa).

The first flight attendants (in the 1930s) were required to be trained in what field?

Nursing. They were there not to serve passengers, but to help those who might become ill during flights.

Sarah, the Duchess of York, penned a line of children's books about a little helicopter named what?

Budgie.

What American pilot became the first to break the sound barrier in 1947 aboard the Bell X-1 rocket-powered aircraft?

Chuck Yeager.

Worried that Australians wouldn't catch that the 1980 comedy film Airplane! *was a spoof, the film was released there under what alternate title?*

Flying High.

What was the name of the plane on which Buddy Holly, J. P. "The Big Bopper" Richardson, and Ritchie Valens were killed?

While some refer to it as *American Pie*, the small craft had no name.

What band's eponymous 1969 album was rejected by many retailers for its suggestive cover, portraying a topless 11-year-old girl holding a phallic model airplane?

Blind Faith.

Of the Boeing 7X7 series airliners (which run from 707 to 787), which can be configured to carry in excess of 500 passengers?

The 747.

Road Signs

What is the name of the standard typeface used on U.S. highway signs?

For many years, those big green freeway signs used a custom style called Highway Gothic. Clearview was declared the new official typeface in 2004, although it will be many years before all existing signs are replaced.

How do authorities determine where to place deer-crossing signs?

There's no set rule. Sadly, they aren't put up in most locations until after an automobile-deer collision occurs.

What are the criteria to get a business listed on one of those "gas-food-lodging" freeway logo boards?

The establishment must be located within 3 miles of the exit; must be open a certain number of hours; and must have telephones, restrooms, and drinking water available.

How are light-up Walk/Don't Walk signs timed?

Traffic engineers traditionally use the 4-feet-per-second rule for walking, so they measure the distance from curb to curb of an intersection, and divide that length by four.

What are the color designations used on these U.S. traffic signs?

◆ *Warning signs?*
Yellow.

◆ *Construction and detour signs?*
Orange.

◆ *Roadway information and directional signs?*
Green.

◆ *Government facilities?*
Brown.

◆ *Nongovernment facilities?*
Blue.

Who makes the decision to post signs like "Bump Ahead"? Why mark one bump and not another?

Such signs are only placed after the local government's highway engineers have done field studies to see if one is warranted. Research has indicated that unnecessary signs distract drivers and cause them to ignore other, more important traffic control devices.

What type of road sign is stolen most often?

Even though unusual street names are common targets, the sign that ends up in the most dorm rooms is perhaps the most dangerous one to go absent: the stop sign.

What's the difference between "Dead End," "No Outlet," and "Not a Through Street"?

As a rule, "Dead End" and "Not A Through Street" both refer to a street that ends without crossing or leading to any other streets. "No Outlet" is usually a road that leads to a maze of other streets and avenues that twist and wind through a subdivision, intersecting only with each other.

World Superlatives

How much taller is the world's tallest mountain, Everest, than the second tallest, K2?

About 750 feet, or less than 3 percent.

How much larger is the world's largest island, Greenland, than the second largest, New Guinea?

Much larger—nearly three times the size. (And, yes, some consider Australia to be an island instead of a "continental land mass.")

How much larger is the world's largest desert, the Sahara, than the second largest, the Arabian?

At more than 3.3 million square miles, the Sahara covers more than three times as much land area as the Arabian.

How much larger is the world's largest ocean, the Pacific Ocean, than the second largest, the Atlantic?

In terms of surface area, the Pacific is a little more than twice the size of the Atlantic.

How much larger is the world's largest lake, the Caspian Sea, than the second largest, Lake Superior?

Despite its name, the Caspian Sea is really a lake, and it's really big. It's nearly five times the size of Lake Superior.

How much longer is the world's longest river, the Nile, than the second longest, the Amazon?

Only about 100 miles longer, or 2 percent of its length. And while the Nile runs for a greater distance, the Amazon carries much more water.

How much taller is the world's tallest waterfall, Angel Falls, than the second tallest, Itatinga?

The upper part of Angel Falls is a little over half a mile high, or 30 percent taller than Itatinga.

Railroads

Why are cabooses no longer commonly seen at the ends of trains?

Blame it on automation. The caboose served as an office for the conductor, flagman, and brakeman. Electronic switches and signaling equipment, coupled with computerized ticketing for passenger trains, have eliminated the need for such a car.

Do train whistles follow any sort of pattern?

Yes. Much like Morse code, trains communicate via their whistle blasts. For example, a sequence of two long blasts, one short blast, and one additional long blast indicates that the train is approaching a crossing.

What is a People Mover?

It is a completely automated transit system that operates on a monorail or duorail and is traditionally found in theme parks, airports, and downtown districts.

What is meant by "light rail"?

A light rail train is an electric railway system that runs underground, on elevated tracks, or on right-of-way railroad tracks.

What do trains have to do with red carpets?

When the New York Central Railroad started its twentieth-century limited luxury train service in 1902, a crimson rug was rolled out to welcome passengers aboard, which is thought to have inspired the phrase "red carpet treatment."

Seen painted on the sides of certain railway cars, what does the phrase "Do Not Hump" mean?

Get your mind out of the gutter. Humping is a way of coupling rail cars together via a man-made incline, or "hump." Letting the car slide down the hump and into another car can jar the contents, however, so fragile loads are safer if not humped.

What exactly is a Pullman car?

It's a luxury sleeping train car invented in 1864. In one of its most famous uses, a Pullman car carried the body of assassinated president Abraham Lincoln from Washington, D.C., to Springfield, Illinois, for burial.

What is train hopping (a.k.a. freight hopping)?

It's the practice of jumping into an empty freight car and riding the rails for free. It's also very dangerous and very illegal.

What were the terminus points of the original Orient Express?

The legendary train service took passengers back and forth from Paris, France, to Istanbul, Turkey. It was cancelled after air travel proved much more convenient.

FUN and GAMES

Bar Games

Why are the felt coverings on most billiard tables green?

Before the game was brought indoors, it was played on grass lawns. When the game moved inside and was brought up to table level (for the benefit of royals, of course), the green grass color was duplicated using felt.

The term ante comes from a Latin word meaning what?

"Before."

"Turkey" is usually a derogatory term for a person, but in bowling, it means you've done something good. What is it?

Rolling three strikes in a row.

Were pinball machines really banned in New York City in the mid-twentieth century?

Yes, they were. From 1942 until 1976, the law prohibited them along with other "gambling machines" that owed more to luck than to skill.

When dealt five cards to begin a poker hand, are the odds better that you'll end up with one pair or with nothing?

Nothing. Of the more than 2.5 million possible hands, 1.3 million are "nothing," while 1.1 million have one pair.

What fictional bowling teams do these sitcom characters belong to?

♦ *Dan Conner* (Roseanne)*?*
  The Wrecking Ballers.

♦ *Ned Flanders* (The Simpsons)*?*
  The Holy Rollers.

♦ *Archie Bunker* (All in the Family)*?*
  The Cannonballers. (Actually, he tried out for the team but didn't make it.)

♦ *Laverne De Fazio* (Laverne & Shirley)*?*
  The Hot Shots/The Big Shots.

♦ *Al Bundy* (Married with Children)*?*
  Gary's Angels.

What Old West marshal was famously shot in the back while holding what became known as the "Dead Man's Hand," aces and eights?

Wild Bill Hickok.

In standard 10-pin bowling, how far is it from the foul line to the center of the head pin?

Sixty feet.

When holding one pair in five-card draw, are your odds of improvement better to draw two cards or three?

Three, always. You're much more likely to get three (or four) of a kind, or two pair, by drawing three cards.

Are there more solid or striped balls in a standard set of billiard balls?

Solid. (There are eight solids and seven stripes.)

What's the suggested maximum number of players in a single-deck poker game?

Seven.

Gottlieb's 1947 **Humpty Dumpty** *pinball game was the first to include what feature?*

Flippers. (In fact, the game had six of them!) These "flipper bumpers" were located in rows on the left and right sides of the machine, and pushed the ball downward instead of upward.

Circuses and Sideshows

Why are circus acts performed inside large rings?

The circular shape enables acts to parade around and be seen by attendees all the way around the ring.

What's the name of the theme music that accompanies a circus?

It's called "Entrance of the Gladiators" and was written at the turn of the twentieth century by Czech composer Julius Fučík.

Are there any locations in America where you can go to the circus (instead of waiting for the circus to come to you)?

Yes, a few. The most famous of these is Circus Circus, a hotel/casino in Las Vegas that also offers amusement-park rides and circus acts under America's largest permanent big top.

Where and when did "Cirque Nouveau" acts originate?

Despite the French name (and the popularity of Cirque du Soleil), the concept dates back to early twentieth-century Russia, where human acts were given precedence over those featuring animals.

Were early circuses traveling events?

No. In ancient Rome, stadiums were built for their specific use. It wasn't until after the fall of Rome that smaller, "portable" circuses made their way around Europe.

Was **Monty Python's Flying Circus** *a real circus?*

No. The circus, like Monty himself, is completely fictional.

Why do Circus Peanuts taste a bit like bananas?

Because banana oil is added to the mixture.

Is there such a place as "clown college"?

Yes. Irvin Feld, who owned the Ringling Brothers/Barnum & Bailey Circus, founded the school in 1968 in Venice, Florida.

Why are circuses no longer performed under the big top?

A combination of serious fires, along with the added expense of transporting and setting up the enormous canvas, made it safer and more cost-effective for circuses to use existing coliseums and arenas.

What patriotic song is the universal circus disaster tune, played to alert employees of an emergency situation?

"Stars and Stripes Forever."

Monopoly

How much cash does each player receive to begin a game of Monopoly?

Exactly $1,500. This is handed out as two $500 bills, two $100 bills, two $50 bills, six $20 bills, five $10 bills, five $5 bills, and five $1 bills.

What property name appears twice on the Monopoly board?

Pennsylvania. It's the name of an avenue (one of the green group) and a railroad.

In the 1970s, Neiman-Marcus offered a limited-edition $600 Monopoly set made out of what?

Chocolate.

Which Monopoly railroad was named after not a train, but an Atlantic City bus service?

The Short Line.

What property on the Monopoly board has always been misspelled?

Marvin Gardens. The actual location in Atlantic City is spelled Marven Gardens.

Why hasn't Monopoly ever been developed into a TV game show?

It was, actually. Merv Griffin created a prime-time version for ABC in 1990, but the rule changes necessary to make the game TV-friendly proved too much for viewers to accept. The show was cancelled after only half a season.

What is the bonus for landing on the Free Parking square?

Nothing, according to the game's standard rules. The fact that some players add money there (when it should go to the bank) extends play and may result in games lasting hours.

The name of what property on the Monopoly board is often mispronounced by players?

Reading Railroad. It's not pronounced like "reading" a book, but like the last name of singer Otis Redding.

Holidays

Which one was originally known as Decoration Day?

Memorial Day.

And speaking of Memorial Day ... what major sporting event is held every Memorial Day weekend?

The Indianapolis 500.

What federal holiday was originally known as Armistice Day?

Veterans' Day.

What's the earliest and latest that Easter Sunday can occur?

It may happen as early as March 22, or as late as April 25.

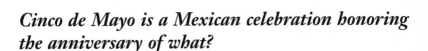

Cinco de Mayo is a Mexican celebration honoring the anniversary of what?

The Battle of Puebla.

Who recorded the original hit versions of these popular holiday radio tunes?

- *New Year: "Same Old Lang Syne"?*
  Dan Fogelberg.

- *St. Patrick's Day: "Wasn't That a Party"?*
  The Irish Rovers.

- *Mother's Day: "I.O.U."?*
  Jimmy Dean.

- *Father's Day: "Cat's in the Cradle"?*
  Harry Chapin.

- *Fourth of July: "Saturday in the Park"?*
Chicago.

- *Halloween: "Monster Mash"?*
Bobby "Boris" Pickett and the Crypt Kickers.

- *Thanksgiving: "Alice's Restaurant"?*
Arlo Guthrie.

- *Christmas: "Happy Xmas (War Is Over)"?*
John Lennon.

In what U.S. city did the first Holiday Inn open its doors in 1952?

Memphis, Tennessee.

In Canada, the Thanksgiving holiday is celebrated in what month of the year?

October (specifically, on the second Monday of the month).

What's the longest-running animated holiday special in TV history?

Rudolph, the Red-Nosed Reindeer, which has aired annually since 1964.

Stupid Human Tricks

Are super-flexible people truly double-jointed?

No. Those stretchy folks have the same number of joints as the rest of us, but the ligaments surrounding those joints are far more lax, which allows for a larger range of motion.

How do ventriloquists throw their voices?

They don't. That's why they work with a dummy, or "figure." The audience focuses on the figure, and the ventriloquist keeps a straight face while manipulating it, so it appears that the dummy is actually talking.

How do those X-ray specs sold in novelty shops enable you to see through things?

They don't. Each "lens" is made of two pieces of cardboard with a feather glued in between them. A quarter-inch hole is punched in each lens, and when the viewer looks through the glasses, light is diffracted by the feather, creating a "double image" and giving the illusion of an X-ray.

Why can't I wiggle my ears?

Genetics. Some folks are able to physically manipulate the auricular muscles (which are attached to a helmetlike scalp tendon), and some aren't. Scientists can't quite explain why.

How can I pull a tablecloth off a table without disturbing the cups and plates on top?

Remember to pull down, not out. Grab the ends of the cloth with two hands, and use a quick, downward jerking motion, as if you were yanking the cloth away from someone.

How strong do you have to be to tear a telephone book in half?

Not very, if you know the trick. You must grip the book at each edge and use your thumbs to push the center down until the book forms a "V" shape. It takes practice, but if you bend the outer edges of the book downward while simultaneously pushing the center down with your thumbs, a crease will form, making it easy to rip through the pages.

Checkers and Chess

How many different pieces are used in the game of chess?

Six: the king, queen, bishop, knight, rook, and pawn.

In checkers, what happens when a player cannot make a legal move?

That player loses the game.

What's the only chess piece that can capture another piece without actually moving on the square it occupies?

The pawn. This maneuver is called "en passant." When a player makes an initial pawn movement of two squares instead of one, his opponent may capture the piece with a pawn as if it had been advanced only one square.

What's the only chess piece that can never move one square at a time?

The knight.

The lyrics of what art-rock band's hit song "Your Move" describe chess pieces and maneuvers?

Yes.

If a checkers player has multiple jumps available, must she choose the move that results in the most captures?

No. While a player must make a jump, the choice of which jump is solely at the discretion of the player.

What card game (named after an Old World bird) shares its name with a chess piece?

Rook.

Which character on **The Cosby Show** *became a checkers whiz and would shout "King me! King me!" when arriving at the back rank?*

Youngest daughter Rudy Huxtable. While skilled at the game, she was such a poor winner that the rest of the family quickly grew tired of playing with her.

Musical Instruments

Of the 88 keys on a piano, how many are black (sharp/flat) and how many are white (natural)?

On most instruments, 36 of the keys are black; the remaining 52 are white.

Who gets the blame ... er, credit ... for inventing the accordion?

Unlike many musical instruments, it's possible to track down the actual "birth certificate" for the accordion. It was patented on May 23, 1829, by Cyrill Demian, an Austrian piano maker.

Was the English horn invented in England?

No, and what's more, it's not even a horn. It's a woodwind instrument similar to an oboe, and was devised in France.

So is the French horn really French?

Yes, and it's really a horn.

What band was portrayed on the famous Saturday Night Live *sketch centered on the musical power of the cowbell?*

Blue Öyster Cult, whose biggest hits were "Don't Fear the Reaper" and "Burnin' for You."

What instrument makes the spooky sounds often heard in 1950s sci-fi and horror films?

The theremin. A similar device was used in The Beach Boys' hit "Good Vibrations."

What are the elements of a basic drum kit?

A bass drum, a snare drum, tom-tom drums (usually three), and cymbals (a ride, a crash, and a hi-hat).

When did the bass guitar replace the upright bass?

In the 1950s, after Leo Fender invented the Precision Bass. Upright basses were unwieldy to transport and difficult to amplify, so Fender's invention quickly took over in the world of popular music.

What's the difference between a violin and a fiddle?

The instruments are one and the same. The difference is in the style of playing. Violinists strive for classical precision, while fiddlers typically play "danceable" music.

Classic Arcade Video Games

Which character on the sitcom Taxi *became so addicted to* Pac-Man *that he began getting his paychecks in quarters?*

Rev. Jim Ignatowski.

Was Donkey Kong *the first hit for Nintendo?*

It was the first video game hit for Nintendo, yes. But Nintendo had been around since 1898, when it was founded as a maker of playing cards.

So is Nintendo the only video-game company that began life doing something else?

No. Another example is Coleco, whose name is an acronym of the company's earlier name: Connecticut Leather Company. The company originally marketed leather goods to shoemakers, and first ventured over into "fun" items by offering leather craft kits featuring popular characters.

What was the name of the "chef" character in the video game **Burgertime**?

Peter Pepper.

What rock band released two albums— Afterburner *and* Eliminator—*that shared their names with arcade video games?*

ZZ Top.

What arcade video game's unusual features included a mock-cursing character, a 45-degree-offset joystick, and a pinball-like "knocker" that would make a loud noise when the player lost?

Q*bert.

What British band's 1982 album, **It's Hard,** *featured the arcade video game* **Space Duel** *on its cover?*

The Who.

What rock band was "digitized" for its own Bally Midway arcade video game in 1983?

Journey.

What 1981 arcade favorite was really five games in one, paving the way for **Tron** *and other similar games?*

Gorf. A player who completed all five "missions" would advance in rank from Space Cadet to Captain, Colonel, and so on.

What early-1980s TV game show allowed kids (or child-parent teams) to compete against each other to reach predetermined scores on video games?

Starcade.

Donkey Kong *spawned many sequels. What was the first?*

Donkey Kong Jr., in 1982.

Evil Otto was the bad guy who showed up in what 1980 Stern game when the player took too long to complete a screen?

Berzerk. The game's eerie robotic voice resonated through arcades with phrases like "Stop the humanoid!" and "Intruder alert!"

Scrabble

The frequency of the letters was based on their appearance in **The New York Times.** *Which letter had to be increased, though, to make the game more "playable"?*

The letter "S."

What symbol appears on the very center square of a Scrabble board?

A black star.

What scoring bonus is given in this center square?

It's pink, meaning it's a double-word score. Red is triple-word score, while light blue and dark blue represent double-letter and triple-letter, respectively.

How many tiles are there in a standard Scrabble game?

One hundred.

What four-letter word contains both of the 10-point tiles in a Scrabble set?

"Quiz."

What are the three most common letters on Scrabble tiles?

In each set of 100 tiles, there are 12 E's, 9 A's, and 9 I's.

How many bonus points does a player earn for using all seven tiles in his or her rack?

Fifty. This play is called a "bingo."

What was the original name of Scrabble?

Lexico.

What rock band got its name when guitarist Dave Peverett used it as a made-up word in a game of Scrabble?

Foghat.

What five letters appear only once in a tile set?

J, K, Q, X, and Z.

A Scrabble player who has no play (or wishes not to make a word) is given what option?

Trading in any or all of his tiles for new ones.

Toys and Games

Were Lincoln Logs invented by Abraham Lincoln?

No, but they were developed by someone kind of famous: John Lloyd Wright, the son of celebrated architect Frank Lloyd Wright.

Was Play-Doh really used as a wallpaper cleaner before it became a kids' modeling clay?

Yes, it's true. It was originally available only in a dull white color.

What are the names of the "dots" on dice and dominoes?

They're called pips. Ask Gladys Knight.

In 1990, what construction toy did NASA use to build a model to illustrate a problem with an antenna on the Hubble Space Telescope?

Tinkertoys.

What new "ailment" was added to the Operation game in 2004?

Brain Freeze. It won in a public vote over Tennis Elbow and Growling Stomach.

Speaking of Operation, what is the name of the game's red-nosed victim ... er, patient?

Cavity Sam.

A Matchbox-brand talking doll of what character was pulled from store shelves in 1989 after parents complained?

Freddy Krueger of the *A Nightmare on Elm Street* films. In a humorous twist, the company had to rely on its other talking doll (Pee Wee Herman) to make up for the loss.

Why is the number seven important when rolling a pair of dice?

For two reasons. First, the number seven is the most common roll, because there are 12 different combinations that can result in a roll of seven. Second, the numbers on opposite sides of a die always total seven.

Does the game Yahtzee have anything to do with yachts?

Yes, in fact. The game was devised by a wealthy Canadian couple who played it aboard their yacht.

First popularized in the 1970s, Hasbro still produces what toy that basically turns kids into a human Lazy Susan?

Sit 'n Spin.

POTPOURRI

Sports Measurements

What's spherical and measures 1.7 inches around?

A golf ball.

What's spherical and measures 2.5 inches around?

A tennis ball.

What's spherical and measures 9 inches around?

A baseball.

What's cylindrical (fooled ya!) and measures 9.5 inches around?

A hockey puck.

What's spherical and measures 12 inches around?

A softball.

What's ellipsoidal (ooh, nice word) and measures 21 inches around the middle?

A football.

What's spherical, light, and measures 27 inches around?

A volleyball.

What's spherical, heavy, and measures 27 inches around?

A bowling ball.

What's spherical and measures 27.5 inches around?

A soccer ball.

What's spherical and measures 30 inches around?

A basketball.

Money

What are the three mint marks that currently appear on U.S. coins?

"D" stands for Denver, "P" for Philadelphia, and "S" for San Francisco (although the last only appears in proof sets).

Why didn't the U.S. mint make the Sacagawea and Presidential series one-dollar coins larger?

Many coin changers were already set for the old Susan B. Anthony dollars, so the new dollars had to maintain the same size and weight. The mint felt that the "gold" tone of the coins would make them much easier to distinguish for consumers.

What two twentieth-century presidents appeared on U.S. coins only a year after their deaths?

Franklin D. Roosevelt (on the dime beginning in 1946) and John F. Kennedy (on the half-dollar beginning in 1964).

What year can you find on pennies, nickels, and dimes, but not on quarters?

1975. That year, the U.S. mint began producing bicentennial quarters, half-dollars, and dollar coins, so those have the dual 1776–1976 date.

How many U.S. currency bills would be in a bundle weighing 1 pound?

490.

What celebrated guitarist is known for using an old British sixpence coin instead of a pick?

Brian May of Queen.

The new presidential one-dollar coins are plated using what alloy?

Brass. That's what gives them their golden tone.

What's the only magnetic coin ever issued by the U.S. mint?

The 1943 steel penny, made to conserve copper for World War II.

How long does a U.S. currency bill "last" before it is replaced?

On average, two to three years.

Are $500 or $1,000 bills worth more than face value?

If they're in decent shape, absolutely. In late 2007, Home Shopping Network offered some 1934-dated samples in extra-fine condition. The $500 bills (with William McKinley's image) went for $1,800, and $1,000 bills (with Grover Cleveland's image) were priced at $3,000.

Actors in Classic TV Commercials

What's the name of the fast-talking spokesman who appeared in several commercials for Federal Express?

John Moschitta.

Who was the Mrs. Olson behind Folger's coffee?

Her name was Virginia Christine, and she hailed from Stanton, Iowa. In fact, the city designed a tribute to their favorite celebrity: the world's largest coffee pot, which is really the local water tower in disguise.

What were the first names of Bartles & Jaymes?

Frank Bartles and Ed Jaymes. Frank spoke, while Ed remained silent. The duo was played by actors David Rufkahr and Dick Maugg.

What character actor who appeared on several sitcoms also portrayed Joe Isuzu on a series of commercials for the Japanese automaker?

David Leisure.

Who reminded us, "Don't squeeze the Charmin!" as Mr. Whipple?

The late actor Dick Wilson. He became so recognizable that a poll taken by Procter & Gamble once placed him as the third most-recognized American, behind Richard Nixon and Billy Graham.

How many actors have portrayed the Maytag repairman on TV over the years?

Three. Known as Ol' Lonely, the Maytag repairman was first portrayed by Jesse White in 1967. Beginning in 1989, Gordon Jump (best known for *WKRP in Cincinnati*) took over the gig. When Jump passed away in 2003, the character disappeared from television until Maytag went on a national search for a replacement. That ended in 2007, when Clay Earl Jackson was given the job.

What actor voiced Sugar Bear in 1960s commercials for the Post cereal known as Sugar Crisp?

Carl Reiner, father of actor/director Rob Reiner and a TV legend in his own right.

Who was Madge the Manicurist, who kept people "soaking in it" with Palmolive?

Jan Miner. While she appeared on Broadway and even performed Shakespeare, she didn't mind that people recognized her as Madge, the role she played for more than a quarter-century.

What star of the classic film The Wizard of Oz *introduced the "Betcha can't eat just one" slogan to America beginning in 1963?*

Bert Lahr, the Cowardly Lion.

Why did the face of Josephine the Plumber, who promoted Comet cleanser, look familiar to many viewers?

They probably remembered Jane Withers from her days as a child actor. She famously roughed up dainty little Shirley Temple in the 1934 film *Bright Eyes*.

Spies and Ghosts

What character works for a boss whose favorite exclamation is "Great Caesar's ghost!"?

Clark Kent, a.k.a. Superman. Kent's boss at *The Daily Planet*, editor Perry White, often used the phrase.

What actor lost a lucrative advertising gig for taking a role as an "undead" character in 1981?

David Naughton. The "Be a Pepper" songster lost his job with the company after appearing in the motion picture *An American Werewolf in London*.

What actor turned down the chance to play James Bond in the 007 film Dr. No, *then went on to play a spy in three TV series*, Danger Man, Secret Agent, *and* The Prisoner?

Patrick McGoohan.

What vocalist successfully sued Ray Parker Jr. because Ray's title theme for the film Ghostbusters *sounded too much like one of his own hits?*

Huey Lewis. Lawyers were able to convince a jury that "Ghostbusters" borrowed too liberally from the Huey Lewis and the News hit "I Want a New Drug."

Boris and Natasha of Rocky & Bullwinkle *fame were spies for what fictional country?*

Potsylvania.

The set of what 1982 horror film was said to be "cursed" when real human remains were used in certain scenes?

Poltergeist. JoBeth Williams revealed the story, although it's unclear if it was true or if she was told this to help her "get into character" for her role in the film.

Consuming all four "ghost monsters" in the original Pac-Man arcade game earns a player how many total points?

3,000 (200 for the first, then 400, 800, and 1,600 for the last). This can only be done after consuming one of the four "energy dots" in the corners of the screen.

In 1996, what spy appeared in the first feature film produced by Nickelodeon?

Harriet the Spy, starring Michelle Trachtenberg.

Is Gene Simmons of rock band KISS the same Gene Simmons who had a novelty hit in the 1960s with "Haunted House"?

No. The earlier singer (sometimes known as "Jumpin' Gene") was from Mississippi, and Gene Simmons was his real name. The KISS bassist was born in Israel as Chaim Witz.

Home Run Hitters

NOTE: The statistics in this section are as of the end of the 2007 season.

Who hit more home runs than anyone else in major league baseball in 1997, but didn't lead either league in the statistic?

Mark McGwire. He hit 58 home runs that year, more than the NL leader (Larry Walker, 49) and the AL leader (Ken Griffey Jr., 56). But because he was traded mid-season from the AL's Oakland Athletics to the NL's St. Louis Cardinals, his total was split between the two leagues.

What MLB player hit more homers than anyone as a first baseman?

Mark McGwire (566).

What MLB player hit more homers than anyone as a second baseman?

Jeff Kent (319).

What MLB player hit more homers than anyone as a shortstop?

Cal Ripken Jr. (345).

What MLB player hit more homers than anyone as a third baseman?

Mike Schmidt (509).

What MLB player hit more homers than anyone as an outfielder?

Barry Bonds (747) (still active as of 2007).

What MLB player hit more homers than anyone as a catcher?

Mike Piazza (396).

What MLB player hit more homers than anyone as a pitcher?

Wes Ferrell (36).

What MLB player hit more homers than anyone as a designated hitter?

Frank Thomas (265) (still active as of 2007).

What MLB player hit more homers than anyone as a pinch hitter?

Cliff Johnson (20).

What MLB player hit more homers than anyone as a switch hitter?

Mickey Mantle (536).

What MLB player hit more homers than anyone for the same franchise?

Hank Aaron (733).

Zoos and Zoo Animals

Do elephants drink through their trunks?

No. They're able to "vacuum up" water into their trunks and then disperse it, but the creatures drink using their mouths just like the rest of us.

What's the largest of the large cats?

Although lions are known as "the kings of beasts," tigers can grow longer—and heavier.

The first zoological park in the United States was Lincoln Park Zoo, which opened its doors in 1868 in what U.S. city?

Chicago.

What European city was home to ...

◆ *... the first private zoo?*
Vienna.

◆ *... the first public zoo?*
Paris.

◆ *... the first zoological gardens to become known by the shortened name "zoo"?*
London.

What San Diego Zoo naturalist has made visits to The Tonight Show *since 1971?*

Joan Embery. She appeared in some hilarious shows with Johnny Carson, and has continued with Jay Leno.

What word for a socially inept person was coined by Dr. Seuss in his book If I Ran the Zoo?

Nerd.

Award Names

The Larry O'Brien Championship Trophy is awarded to the winner of what pro sports event?

The National Basketball Association finals.

What well-known trophy was named after Frederick Arthur?

The Stanley Cup. Arthur was better known as Lord Stanley of Preston.

The NFL Most Valuable Player Award is named after what football legend?

Jim Thorpe.

What Major League Baseball pitcher won the most games without ever winning the Cy Young Award?

Why, Cy Young. He won 511 games in the major leagues.

The Jules Rimet Trophy is better known by what name?

The World Cup (of soccer ... er, football).

The Siemens Trophy is presented to the winner of what collegiate event?

The NCAA Men's basketball tournament.

What's the proper name of the trophy presented to the winning team of pro baseball's World Series?

The Commissioner's Trophy.

What school has given out the Pulitzer Prize since 1917?

Columbia University. The college's journalism school was founded using money that publisher Joseph Pulitzer left in his will.

What's the rather lengthy full name of the Tony Awards?

The Antoinette Perry Awards for Excellence in Theatre.

The Hugo Awards are presented annually to the best works in what field of literature and art?

Science-fiction and fantasy.

Which Nobel Prize was first awarded in 1969?

The Economics medal. The other five—Chemistry, Literature, Medicine/Physiology, Peace, and Physics—have been around since 1901.

Six Degrees of Sitcoms

What actor passed on Gilligan's Island *to star in* My Mother the Car?

Jerry Van Dyke. Unfortunately for him, it was more than 20 years later before he finally found a role in a second hit sitcom: *Coach*, on which he portrayed Luther Van Dam.

So was his decision to turn down that role the worst decision a sitcom actor ever made?

It's close, but the award might go to Mickey Rooney. He was penciled in to portray Archie Bunker in *All in the Family*, but felt that the role was "too rough" for TV audiences. The role went to Carroll O'Connor instead.

Speaking of Carroll O'Connor, didn't he write the theme song for All in the Family?

No, but he was credited with co-writing the show's closing song, "Remembering You." In truth, he penned lyrics to the song (which were never used). Because he was credited as co-writer, O'Connor received a royalty payment every time an episode was broadcast.

Maude *was a spin-off of* All in the Family. *Did the two-part "abortion" episode really cause a furor when it was first aired?*

There was a reaction, yes, but it was mild compared to what happened when the network repeated the show that summer. Producers hadn't known what to expect during the first airing, but when it was due to repeat, pressure from viewers, advertisers, and clergymen forced several CBS affiliates to nix the broadcast.

Bea Arthur of Maude *also starred in* The Golden Girls. *Who was the oldest of that aged quartet?*

It seems logical to assume that Estelle Getty, who portrayed Sophia (Dorothy's mother), was the senior member of the cast. But in fact, Getty is a year younger than Arthur. The most golden of *The Golden Girls* was actually Betty White, born in January 1922.

But Betty White's first major role was as sultry Sue Ann Nivens on The Mary Tyler Moore Show, *right?*

Actually, she juggled two shows in the early 1950s: her own talk show (*The Betty White Show*) and the title role in a sitcom known as *Life with Elizabeth*.

Mary Tyler Moore got her start on TV as wife Laura Petrie on **The Dick Van Dyke Show.** *Hey, was he ...?*

Yes, Dick Van Dyke and the aforementioned Jerry Van Dyke are related. They're brothers.

Magic

How many different answers can appear on the original Magic 8-Ball?

Twenty. The 20-sided polyhedron inside the ball is called an icosahedron.

What's the last name of Sabrina the Teenage Witch?

Spellman. The same name was used in the comic books, in the 1970s animated series, and in the 1990s–2000s TV show and cartoon.

What magician changed his last name from Cotkin (just for the "Dickens" of it)?

David Copperfield.

What type of dove do magicians usually use in their acts?

They prefer female ringneck doves, because they are mostly fluff and their feathers can easily be compressed to fit into a jacket pocket. They also make less noise than male doves.

What do magicians usually refer to as their most important tool?

Stage patter. A good magician keeps up a running commentary as he sets up his tricks, throws in lots of corny jokes, and singles out members of the audience. This keeps the crowd's attention on his words, and not on his hands—until he wants them to watch his hands, that is.

What was unusual about the names of the two actors who portrayed Darrin Stephens on TV's Bewitched?

Both had the same first name: Dick York and Dick Sargent.

Why do magicians often wear tuxedos?

They started out wearing formal gear back in the days when people dressed up for a night at the theater. It was a way of being perceived as a professional, and not strictly an entertainer.

What is "roughing spray"?

An aerosol adhesive used by magicians to temporarily glue certain playing cards back to back to facilitate tricks.

Sports Team Names

What are the only four teams to keep the same city-and-name combination every season since the NL and AL joined up to form Major League Baseball in 1901?

The Chicago White Sox, the Detroit Tigers, the Pittsburgh Pirates, and the St. Louis Cardinals.

What Pennsylvania university's teams are known by three nicknames: the Brown and White, the Engineers, and the Mountain Hawks?

Lehigh. The Mountain Hawks name was introduced in 1995, but the school still makes use of all three monikers.

What's the only U.S. state whose name applies to teams in all four major league sports (MLB, NBA, NFL, and NHL)?

Minnesota. There's baseball's Twins, basketball's Timberwolves, football's Vikings, and hockey's Wild.

What other state names are used for pro sports teams?

- ◆ Arizona (Cardinals, Diamondbacks).

- ◆ Colorado (Avalanche, Rockies).

- ◆ Florida (Marlins, Panthers).

- ◆ Indiana (Pacers).

- ◆ New Jersey (Devils, Nets).

- ◆ Tennessee (Titans).

- ◆ Texas (Rangers).

- ◆ Utah (Jazz).

And here are also three less-specific references:

- ◆ Golden State (Warriors).

- ◆ Carolina (Hurricanes, Panthers).

- ◆ New England (Patriots).

The Cleveland Barons and Kansas City Scouts were once members of what professional sports league?

The National Hockey League. Both teams lasted only two seasons (1974–1976).

What NFL team never "moved," yet played home games in three different states during the 1970s?

The New York Giants. They played in New York until 1973, then two seasons in New Haven, Connecticut, followed by another season in New York before settling in East Rutherford, New Jersey, in 1976.

Similarly, what pro baseball team has had four different names despite never leaving the state?

The Angels. Originally enfranchised in 1961 as the Los Angeles Angels, the team was renamed the California Angels in 1966 and the Anaheim Angels in 1996. Then, in 2005, the club became the Los Angeles Angels of Anaheim. That's a mouthful!

What pro sports franchises currently share team names?

♦ Cardinals: St. Louis (MLB) and Arizona (NFL).

♦ Panthers: Carolina (NFL) and Florida (NHL).

♦ Rangers: Texas (MLB) and New York (NHL).

♦ Kings: Sacramento (NBA) and Los Angeles (NHL).

♦ Giants: San Francisco (MLB) and New York (NFL).

Broadway and the Theatre

What exactly is Broadway?

It is the oldest north-south thoroughfare in New York City. It runs the length of Manhattan, from Inwood to Bowling Green, and was built over a Native American pathway known as the Wickquasgeck Trail.

How many Broadway theaters are there?

There are 40, but only 5 (Broadway Theatre, Circle in the Square, Marquis, Palace, and Winter Garden) are actually located on the famed street. Any auditorium located in the theater district with a seating capacity 500-plus is categorized as a Broadway theater.

What is the difference between "Off-Broadway" and "Off-Off Broadway"?

If a theater has 100 to 499 seats, it is considered Off-Broadway. Off-Off-Broadway theaters either have 99 seats or less, or mount shows using nonequity (nonunion) actors and workers.

What's the British equivalent of Broadway?

The West End, which is home to London's theatre district.

Why is it called "The Great White Way"?

The term dates back to 1901, when a blizzard hit New York and the city was blanketed with snow. In his editorial, a Texas-born *New York Telegraph* writer referred to the wintry tableau outside his office window as a "Great White Way." Once Broadway became a prime theater district, the glowing white lights on marquees kept the nickname alive.

What is the longest-running show in Broadway history?

On January 9, 2006, Andrew Lloyd Webber's *Phantom of the Opera* marked its 7,486th performance, topping the previous record-holder, *Cats*.

Miscellany

Chubby Checker earned his name as a parody of sorts of what other early rock legend?

Fats Domino. The suggestion came from Bobbie Clark, wife of *American Bandstand*'s Dick Clark.

What makes certain insects (like bees) "buzz"?

It's the rapid action of their wings against the air that creates the sound.

Will a staple in a food container in a microwave oven cause a spark/fire/explosion?

No. Experts say that a staple or two doesn't contain enough metal to cause "arcing" or damage to a microwave oven or its contents, as long as it's not touching the walls on the inside of the oven.

Who ranks higher, a U.S. Army captain or a U.S. Navy captain?

The Navy captain. It's an O-6 level, or the equivalent of an Army colonel. The Army's captain is an O-3, like a Navy lieutenant.

Well, then, who ranks higher, a U.S. Army lieutenant or a U.S. Navy lieutenant?

Again, it's the Navy. A Navy lieutenant is an O-3, while an Army lieutenant (First Lieutenant) is an O-2.

How can a woman traveling from the United States to Britain via plane go up a whole dress size during the flight?

Well, one way is by overloading on the complimentary bags of peanuts. But practically, the reason is that dress sizes run a unit higher in Britain. (A woman who's a size 16 in New York would be a size 18 in London).

What vegetable did Mark Twain call "a cabbage with a college education"?

Cauliflower.

Henry the Navigator is best known as a Portuguese prince who explored what part of the world?

Actually, none. He arranged and mapped—but didn't participate in—several journeys down the western coast of Africa.

What 1960s TV sidekick's skin-tight garb led to complaints from the Catholic League of Decency?

Robin, as portrayed by Burt Ward on the campy 1960s version of *Batman*. His autobiography was appropriately titled *My Life in Tights*.

From 1967 to 1973, which three musical acts won two Record of the Year Grammy awards each?

The Fifth Dimension, Simon and Garfunkel, and Roberta Flack.

What type of creature was the title character in the book Flowers for Algernon?

A mouse.

*What's the name of the rodeo event in which a
rider on a horse distracts a calf from a herd and
works to keep it in place?*

Cutting.

*The owner of the Bristol Motor Speedway offered
millions of dollars in a failed attempt to draw what
event to the interior of the facility's track?*

A college football game (between Tennessee and Virginia Tech).

*The carnivorous plant known as the venus flytrap
is native to what continent?*

North America. It only grows naturally along the coastlines of
North and South Carolina.

*Is the Wesson who invented Wesson oil also the one
behind Smith & Wesson firearms?*

No. Daniel Wesson joined up with Horace Smith in the 1850s,
and devised the first repeating rifle. David Wesson developed a
process for treating cottonseed oil in 1899, and the product (first
known as Snowdrift) later took his name.

What are the only four gemstones that are not minerals?

Amber, coral, jet, and pearl.

Which is taller, the Washington Monument or the Great Pyramid of Cheops?

The Washington Monument is 555 feet in height, compared to 481 feet for the Great Pyramid.

How many years did Julius Caesar serve as emperor of Rome?

None. Rome had no emperors until after his death. Gaius Octavius, Julius Caesar's grandnephew, became the first Roman emperor (under the name Caesar Augustus) in 27 B.C.E.

Can a "Friday the thirteenth" occur in consecutive months?

It can, and does on occasion. On nonleap years when February 13 is on a Friday, March 13 is also on a Friday.

Can a tarantula kill a human?

No. The spider's bite is painful, but not lethal.

The British sometimes use the unit "stone" to reference weight. How much is a stone?

Fourteen pounds. That means that a svelte 98-pounder would weigh 7 stones, a 150-pound person would rank about 11 stones, and a 220-pound linebacker would carry about 16 stones.

Hee-Haw *made a bold statement in 1969 by inviting what African American singer to appear on the show's premiere episode?*

Charley Pride.

What TV boss was known in different episodes as Harry, Oscar, Sam, and Seymour?

Fred Flintstone's superior, Mr. Slate.

Is it true that "every rose has its thorn"?

No, in fact. Those painfully sharp points on the stems of roses are spines, not true thorns.

What was the first Ronco device invented and offered by Ron Popeil?

The Pocket Fisherman.

What two motion pictures include a scene in which a rabbit is attacked with a hand grenade?

It's amazing that this happened once (let alone twice). The most famous is probably in *Monty Python and the Holy Grail*. The other is *Raising Arizona*.